THE
DIGITAL
VIDEOMAKER'S
GUIDE

KATHRYN SHAW WHITVER

Published by Michael Wiese Productions, 4354 Laurel Canyon Blvd., Suite 234, Studio City, CA 91604, (818) 379-8799, Fax (818) 986-3408.

Cover design by Art Hotel, Los Angeles.
Copyediting by Robin Quinn.

Printed by Braun-Brumfield, Inc., Ann Arbor, Michigan.
Manufactured in the United States of America.

Printed on recycled stock.

ISBN 0-941188-21-3

Whitver, Kathryn Shaw,
    The digital videomaker's guide / by Kathryn Shaw Whitver.
        p.   cm.
    Includes bibliographical references (p.   )
    ISBN 0-941188-21-3 : $24.95
    Digital video. I. Title. II. Title: Digital video maker's guide.
TK6680.5.W48   1995
791.45'023-dc20   94-48307
                                    CIP

ACKNOWLEDGMENTS

Many thanks to Mr. Ken Davis, Mr. Steve Kroeze, and Mr. Jeff Niedermayer of OptImage for their technical expertise and careful editing of the material in this book. Their generosity and remarkable talent for explaining complex processes in understandable terms has helped MPEG developers all over the world, and their skill and knowledge permeate each page of this book. As development engineers in MPEG encoding, Steve, Ken, and Jeff were key members of the engineering team that brought one of the first MPEG encoding systems to market in 1992 and their work today continues to expand the boundaries of MPEG technology.

Author's Note

Digital Video is a techno-buzzword that has unfortunately become more ambiguous with each passing day. This book is focused on one format: MPEG-compressed, full-motion, full-screen digital video. Until very recently, digital-motion video meant tiny video windows and lurching motion. Audio was difficult to synchronize and often could not be played at all.

MPEG-compressed motion video brings full-screen, VHS-quality video and stereo sound to the digital world and leads the way to new computer applications and home entertainment possibilities. MPEG-digital video files can be stored on computer hard drives and CDs, or transmitted without lost quality over telephone and TV cable lines. It is this format that is the basis for the union of computers with television for interactive TV. MPEG-digital video is the only format that can cross over from the computer to the home entertainment center and still meet the high quality demands of the movie-viewing public.

For those of you entering the digital video market, I hope this book provides you with some valuable insight and helps you along your path. It's an exciting world and I wish you much success. That said, please read on....

Kathryn

TABLE OF CONTENTS

Introduction   3

Markets for Digital Video   7
    Infotainment/Entertainment   10
    Home Entertainment   11
    Home Video Editing and Production   12
    Feature Length Movies   13
    Self-Improvement and How-To Videos   13
    Music Videos   14
    Computer-Based Applications   14
    Education and Professional Training   15
    Point of Information and Point of Sale   17

Digital Video Platforms   21
    Video CD   24
    CD-i   25
    CD-ROM   26
    Games Platforms   27
    Interactive TV   27

The Production Team   31
    Producer   34
    Marketing Manager   34
    Content Expert   35
    Audio/Video Producer   35
    Art Director/Artist   36
    Project Manager   37

Digital Video Engineer   38
Application Designer/Programmer   38
Testers   40
Teamwork   41

The Digital Video Studio   43
A/V Equipment   48
Computer Hardware   50
Computer Software   53

The Process   55
Analyze   59
Design   64
Produce   68
Create   80
Validate   86

Launching Your Title   91
Product Packaging   93
Copyrights   94
Duplication   95
Distribution   95

Technical Notes   99
MPEG Explained   101
Digital Compression   103
Common Problems   109
MPEG1 and MPEG   111

Techniques and Effects   115
Interactivity   115
Fast Branching   115

Audio Techniques and Multilingual Audio   117
Seamless Branching   118
Forward and Reverse Scanning   121

Types of Encoding Systems   123
The High End   125
Mid-Range Systems   125
Low Budget Options   126
Making Your Selection   127

Words of Wisdom from Two MPEG Experts   129
From Mr. Bob Auger   131
From Mr. David Cunningham   132
From Mr. Dieter Schleutmann   132

The Color Books   135
Compact Disk Architecture   138
CR-ROM   139
Mixed Mode   141
CD-ROM XA   142
Hybrid   143
CD-i   144
CD-i Bridge   145
Video CD   146
3DO   148
Disc Mastering   148
Interleaving and Multiplexing   150
More Information   151

Interactive TV   153

Resources   161

Education and Training   163
Digital Video Systems and Software Companies   164
Digital Video Services   167
Playback Hardware for MPEG Digital Video   171

Digital Video Title Case Study   173
Analyze   176
Design   177
Produce   177
Create   178
Validate   179
Wrap-up   180
Budgeting Information   181

Digital Video Titles   185
Movies   187
Music Videos   188
Games   188
Special Interest   189
Education and Training   189

CD-ROM Developers   191

Recommended Reading   231
Specifications   233
Magazine Articles   233
Other Works   234

Glossary   235

Books Available from MWP   245

INTRODUCTION

INTRODUCTION

Digital video is a hot topic. Nearly every computer and multimedia magazine you look at today is debating what you can and cannot do with full-screen, full-motion digital video. The jargon is new and impressive, and it's difficult to know what's real, what's fantasy, what is likely to be achieved, and what is just so much hype from an excited industry.

With high-quality video, and near CD-quality audio, there's a lot of reasons to be excited. Old film archives transferred to compact disc are virtually immune to degeneration and simple to store. Movies on compact disc have the same basic controls as a VCR player, but allow viewers to jump quickly from beginning to end or anywhere in between without waiting for a tape to wind. Since CDs are a random access medium, viewers of interactive movies can determine which direction they want the story to go by making choices at different plot points as the movie progresses. Interactive TV and video on demand services are possible because of digital video technology.

Leaders in multimedia and digital video technology such as John Hawkins of Philips NV expect digital video (VideoCD) to revolutionize the film and video industry in the same ways that audio CDs changed the face of the audio industry, and for the same reasons: higher quality, great durability, and lower costs for production, storage, and distribution.

Home entertainment is one of the biggest markets for digital video. Consumer electronics giants like Philips, JVC, Magnavox, Samsung, Goldstar, Yashica, and Panasonic are marketing players for digital video or have modified existing multimedia players to play MPEG digital video. Developers are working at full capacity to convert existing movies to digital video formats, and to produce new digital video only titles for market.

Professional training CDs combine traditional interactive training and digital video to provide students with realistic views of processes and techniques when hands-on training is not practical or possible. Interactive multimedia has the potential to redefine home entertainment from passive viewing to active involvement with the television set. But multimedia developers knew that still video pictures and animations could not compete with the realism consumers were accustomed to from TV. Motion video in a digital format was needed before interactive multimedia could honestly move from the personal computer to the living room.

Digital video technology is rapidly changing and growing. MPEG compression has been accepted as the *defacto* world standard for digital video playback. When the first compression hardware and software were introduced in 1993, it took 120 hours to convert 1 hour of video tape to a full-screen, full-motion digital video. One year later, real-time encoding systems enabled production teams to convert that same 1 hour of video tape to digital video in just 1 hour. Engineering teams are now focused on making that conversion process faster, cheaper, and easier, with improved video quality. The third generation of digital video systems will allow digital video developers to load a tape in one machine, a CD blank in another, and click one button to launch a total tape-to-disc transfer.

In this book, we'll explore the creation of MPEG digital video titles from concept to finished application. We'll discuss:

- **The Management Process**
  How to build a production team,
  The life cycle of a digital video project,
  Choosing a delivery platform,
  Legal rights and responsibilities, and
  Leveraging your investment in a new technology.

- **The Technology Processes**
  What is digital video?
  What are the different formats of digital video?
  How video is captured and produced?
  What types of scenes are easy to digitize, and what makes a scene difficult?
  How are some of these difficulties overcome?

- **The Production Process**
  Authoring,
  Making a disc or tape,
  Marketing your ideas, and
  Marketing your titles.

The excitement over digital video is warranted. The arguments of stable and lasting quality and durability were resolved years ago when audio compact discs made their mark on the audio industry. Digital video goes far beyond those advantages and will drastically change the way we entertain, learn, work, and live.

Digital video has the potential to reshape the television and entertainment industry in remarkable ways. During the next few years, consumers will define the boundaries of interactive television technology, and fortunes will be made and lost in the process.

Understanding digital video technology and taking advantage of its uniqueness is the foundation on which success or failure in this new industry will be defined. Quality of production will be judged without compromise against traditional analog devices like VHS, and viewers are not likely to accept low quality patiently while the technology matures. Developers who take the time now to become educated in production techniques and encoding processes will be able to produce high-quality digital video with exciting interactive elements with their first market entries. Developers who produce digital video programs that can cross over to other platforms will be able to leverage their investment, expand their market, and provide value-added services to their viewing audiences.

MARKETS FOR DIGITAL VIDEO

MARKETS FOR DIGITAL VIDEO

Digital video is loosely categorized as a multimedia format. While reliable predictions concerning the digital video market are not available, we can look at the multimedia market as an indicator. The digital video market is also represented, in part, by the VCR/home entertainment markets. We'll look at both markets as we explain where digital video fits in.

The current markets for multimedia can be broadly classified into six segments: Infotainment, education, business, professional training, point of information/point of sale, and publishing. Based on data from Frost and Sullivan[1], these six markets have been broken down in a pie chart, provided on page 10.

The chart forecasts the markets for the six multimedia subject areas in 1997 and represents worldwide revenues of $23.2 billion. Over a 9 year time span from 1989 to 1997, this multimedia market enjoys a compound growth rate of more than 25% per year, according to Frost and Sullivan.

Of these six multimedia markets, entertainment, training, and point of information/point of sale have received the most attention from digital video developers.

Beyond the multimedia classification, Video CD expands the digital video market into home entertainment and challenges the current video tape market with linear movie titles.

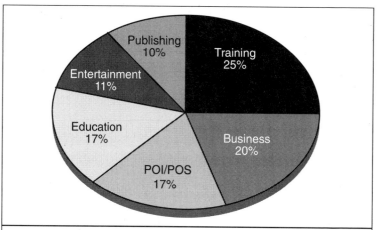

Source: *Frost and Sullivan - 1993 World Multimedia Application Market*

Infotainment/Entertainment

Digital video is the single most important breakthrough in multimedia for home entertainment since *Pong*. While debates continue to revolve around Sega/Nintendo/3DO/CD-i and which is the best home entertainment system, the manufacturers of each of these systems have quietly agreed that MPEG digital video is crucial to the long-term success of each and have announced or released MPEG capabilities for their players. At the same time, Video CD players have emerged to challenge the 100 million strong VCR market.

Home Entertainment

The VCR market encompasses music videos, exercise videos, feature films, and information (how-to) videos. Videos for home entertainment offer several distinct and clear advantages over video tape when delivered on a CD:

FEATURES	CD	VHS TAPE
MULTI-PURPOSE PLAYER	YES	NO
DURABILITY OF RECORDED MEDIUM	NON-DEGRADABLE	DEGRADES WITH EACH PLAY
PRODUCTION COSTS (MASS PRODUCTION)	ABOUT $1.00/DISC	ABOUT $4.00/TAPE
SCAN/SEEK/FORWARD/ REVERSE	IMMEDIATE ACCESS/ PRODUCT INDEXED	WAIT FOR TAPE TO WIND/REWIND. NOT INDEXED
INTERACTIVE	YES[2]	NO
AUDIO QUALITY	CD-QUALITY	BROADCAST STEREO

The current biggest disadvantage to using CD over video tape is that a CD holds about 72 minutes of digital audio and video. A feature length movie requires two CDs. This disadvantage is being addressed with the development of multi-disc players that allow you to load several CDs at a time and switch CDs as needed, quickly and seamlessly. Double, triple, and higher density discs are also being developed by researchers in compact disc technology and may soon offer the ability to store even several feature-length movies on a single CD.

Home Video Editing and Production

Since the first consumer camera was introduced, families have been recording their life and times in pictures. Home movie cameras added a new dimension to this pastime, then video cameras hit the market with sound, higher quality, and hours of recording rather than minutes. Many small companies have been founded since the early '80s that transfer film and slides to video tape.

Digital video offers similar opportunities. It's a fairly simple procedure to transfer film, slides or photos, and home-recorded video tape to CD. Digitizing still video pictures is a simple and well-defined process. Easy and low-cost editing software for video tape is available for personal computers. Film and video tape can be digitally encoded, and multimedia software provides a way to mix all these elements and add audio. When recorded to a CD, the family now has all their history on a single viewing platform that will look as good to their grandkids as it does the day it is recorded.

Video CDs are not likely to replace the VCR and camera for a long time, at least not until home recording on CDs is an affordable alternative to VHS tape. But they can offer consumers a new level of quality in home-recorded movies. Service bureaus that cater to the home movie-maker can edit video tape and combine footage from many tapes. Then they can add some special effects, still photos, and title screens to create high-quality Video CD titles from a home library. The concept is simple, and very much like collecting photo negatives and having a photo service enlarge and reprint your best photographs. Kodak already offers this service on CDs for still photos with their PhotoCD format. Video CD carries this out two steps further with movies and audio.

Feature Length Movies

Feature movies are easily converted to digital video CD. A master tape is digitally encoded, the on-screen controls for the user are added, then a disc is mastered and replicated. Paramount began building a library of popular movies on CD in 1993. Among the first were the enormously popular *Top Gun*, *Hunt for Red October*, and *Planes, Trains and Automobiles*. Other studios such as Columbia/ TriStar, MCA, and Thorne/EMI have announced support for digital video CDs, and MGM/United Artists have reached an agreement with Philips Media Electronic Publishing to release 30 classic films on CD. Considering the investment movie fans have in video tape, the durability and quality offered by digital video CDs becomes a very attractive advantage to consumers.

Self-Improvement and How-To Videos

Exercise videos when delivered from a digital video CD are easily customized to the viewer's needs. A single digital video CD can be viewer-programmed with a menu to deliver, for example, 10 minutes of warm-up, 20 minutes of low-impact aerobics, and 10 minutes of cool-down for one viewer, and 7 minutes of warm-up, 25 minutes of strength training, 10 minutes of flexibility, and 8 minutes of cool-down for another viewer.

How-to videos on CD eliminate some of the biggest irritations of video tape. Picture quality does not suffer when a digital video CD is stopped. A zoom function can be added to selected frames so viewers can look up close at a particular woodworking joint or pattern placement. The structure of a how-to video is more conducive to learning as certain scenes can branch to a more detailed segment at the viewer's discretion.

Music Videos

Music videos have brought live concerts into our living rooms. What these videos lacked was the quality of audio that we've come to expect in music, and the ability to play only our favorite songs or even to simply scramble the order of play. Digital video on CD combines the best of music video and audio CD. By connecting a pair of good stereo speakers to your TV or digital video player, you have a CD-quality, stereo-audio concert video, and you can program the order of play just like on your audio CD player.

Computer-Based Applications

In addition to these, digital video clips can be included in traditional computer-based home education materials. Video encyclopedias can include actual footage of the moon landing, World War II battles, cells dividing under a microscope, and video visits to underwater volcanoes. Events once captured only in a still picture will come to life as digital video encyclopedias occupy our home libraries. Computer games can take on unmatched realism and even provide "real" opponents to challenge users.

learning experiences by providing realistic feedback to students and helping them develop their own analysis skills.

According to research conducted by Dr. Ben Roach of the Association for Managerial, Professional, and Executive Development,[3] learning effectiveness can be quantified according to teaching methods. When students learn by auditory means such as lecture or audio tape, about 20% of the material is retained. When video is added, such as video tape, retention increases to 40%. When students learn interactively, such as in labs or by interactive optical media, retention jumps to a remarkable 80%. Digital video enhances the interactive learning experience by providing a realistic environment for presenting information and allowing the student to participate actively in their own success.

Add-on equipment such as printers and external disk drives can be connected to some multimedia players to allow teachers to set up student records and store test results. Teachers can monitor and evaluate students' learning processes and adjust future projects based on quantifiable data that demonstrates the effectiveness of various CD applications.

Point of Information and Point of Sale

Have you ever looked at an item in a catalog and wished you could look at the back, look at the inside, or see it in a different color? With digital video and point of sales discs, you can do all that. The enormous storage capacity and high-quality video of CDs can provide shoppers with information about items that helps make long-distance decisions easy.

The Sears and Roebuck catalog, a staple in American households for over a hundred years, is no longer being printed simply because the cost of printing and mailing a color catalog is not practical in an increasingly competitive retail market. If that same information can be published at $1 to $2 per copy and delivered for 52 cents, more companies could afford to print catalogs and the savings can be passed along to both consumers and investors. Digital video clips take information presented on still pictures a step further and actually bring home shopping TV into homes at the customer's convenience. By making this type of shopping available to consumers at any time, there are no competing shows and customers watch when they're in the mood to buy.

Realty companies can take advantage of the portability of CDs and produce discs that allow home buyers to shop for homes by viewing digital video clips from a single office or their home, narrowing choices based on high-quality information before actually visiting the home for their final decisions. Because CDs are inexpensive to produce even in small numbers and can be quickly produced in a matter of days, information is updated quickly and in a changing market. Realtors can take a CD and portable player to a buyer or a client interested in leasing and review the market at their customer's place of business. In addition to a digital video tour of the home or office, the CD can also contain information screens that list the property and building specifics.

Point of information kiosks like tourism centers can take advantage of digital video CDs by offering visitors a virtual library of area information. Digital video clips can show activities or events taking place just like video tape, while random access allows viewers to choose information from a table of contents. Printed brochures that back up the video material can displayed on the kiosk so that visitors can take maps, schedules, and other important printed information with them.

[1]Frost & Sullivan, *World Multimedia Application Markets*, 1993.
[2] Level of interactivity is dependant on delivery platform. See platforms section for more information.
[3] *Interactive Optical Technologies in Education and Training*, Ben Roach, Ph.D., © 1992, AMPED.

DIGITAL
VIDEO
PLATFORMS

DIGITAL VIDEO PLATFORMS

Remember the VHS/Beta race of the early 80's? Remember the personal computer race of the mid-to-late 80's? Remember the games machine race of the entire 80's and early 90's? That one is not over yet. The biggest irritation in each of these battles is that consumers have to make choices between platforms that are not compatible. Choosing one platform means rejecting another. Worse yet, choosing a platform that is technologically superior does not ensure that you are buying the winning platform, and thousands of people are stuck with systems that are passé before their time.

Back when audio CDs were introduced, consumers were given an enormous break when Philips and Sony collaborated to write the "Red Book" specification. Basically, the Red Book specified how an audio CD was recorded, formatted, and played back, and this specification ensured that every audio CD would be playable on any audio CD player. Consumers then could choose any brand of CD player based on their own set of criteria without concern about audio CD formats.

That same break is being given to the digital video industry. First, full-screen, full-motion digital video was defined in ISO 11172 and later adopted by the Motion Picture Experts Group (MPEG). Lessons of the past were learned, and hardware and software manufacturers were quick to adopt the MPEG standard for digital video. Now, any playback hardware that is MPEG compliant will play any digital video clip produced to the MPEG standard.

There are several platforms today that are capable of MPEG digital video playback. Several others have announced plans for MPEG support.

Video CD

Video CD is defined by the "White Book" standard. It consists of MPEG video and optional high-resolution still video screens in 98 separate tracks. Video CDs may contain "chapter marks" that allow viewers to jump to specific points in the video, much like chapters in a book. Video CDs also contain a CD-i application that allows all Video CDs to be played in CD-i players equipped with MPEG circuitry. The White Book is actually an expansion of the Red Book so Video CD players also have the advantage of being able to play all existing audio CDs.

Video CD players are relatively new in the market but are receiving great media attention and predictions of market success are dramatic. Several companies, such as JVC, Digital Video Systems, and Samsung, are manufacturing dedicated Video CD players and plan extensive

US product launches in 1995. Video CD playback boards for personal computers are available worldwide, as are Video CD upgrades to popular CD-based games platforms and CD-i. These add-in boards and player updates provide a broad installed base for Video CDs even before the entrance of dedicated Video CD players to the market.

Since the Video CD player is considered to be a competitor to video cassette, marketing professionals use the audio tape vs. CD paradigm to base market predictions for the acceptability of Video CD. Since the White Book specification detailing the Video CD is actually just an elaboration of the audio CD specification, audio CD players can be upgraded to full Video CD capability with the addition of the video decoder circuits. This upgrade, when made available to general consumers, is likely to cost around $100.

CD-i

CD-i, Compact Disc-interactive, was introduced to consumers in the fall of 1991 with the prime target group being family-based entertainment. CD-i is a self-contained multimedia player that connects to a TV set. CD-i offers high-quality still video, full-motion, full-screen digital video, and near CD-quality stereo audio with full interactivity. Additionally, CD-i players are Video CD-, Photo CD-, and Audio CD-compatible, which greatly broadens its consumer appeal as a versatile and inexpensive home entertainment device.

25

At the end of 1994, about 1 million CD-i players had been sold for homes and businesses around the world. The library of titles includes 200 consumer titles including encyclopedia and home reference, instructional/tutorial, games for children and adults, and about 40 feature movies. The library of corporate training, client education, and point of information/point of sale titles numbers more than 400. Executives at Philips, the major manufacturer of CD-i players, estimates the market to grow to 3 million players sold by the end of 1996.

CD-ROM

CD-ROM is a computer-based platform that is essentially a storage device that is accessed through a personal computer. Approximately 30% of American households have a personal computer, and most businesses use computers. The newest computers offered to consumers are multimedia PCs that include a CD-ROM drive and stereo speakers. The volume and type of information offered on CD-ROM is immense, ranging from encyclopedias, telephone directories, catalogs, and game collections, to the newest interactive multimedia presentations.

Personal computers equipped with a CD-ROM drive and an MPEG playback card can take advantage of full-screen, full-motion digital video. Video CDs can be played but, depending on the manufacture of the MPEG card, may need to contain a platform specific software application to provide the control panel. Video CDs that do not contain a computer application can still play the video, but the controls may not be present.

Games Platforms

CD-based games platforms, including Atari's Jaguar, 3D0, CD-i, and Commodor CD32, all support the MPEG standard for digital video. One of the biggest advances in game development has been the increasing realism of the graphics. With the addition of MPEG digital video, the realism is no longer dependent on quality and depth of computer generated graphics. Real backgrounds and actual scenery can be filmed and converted to MPEG digital video in the same way that movie scenes are shot, then integrated into the game environment.

The addition of MPEG support to the games platforms also allows users to play (with some limitations) digital video clips from previously incompatible platforms. For example, when you put a digital video CD-i disc into a CD32 player, the CD32 player recognizes and plays the digital video clips from the CD-i disc. The "foreign" disc may not display the video control panels, but linear movies will play from start to finish and manual control may be available.

Interactive TV

Although interactive TV is not specifically CD-based, a

discussion here is applicable since this medium is dependent on MPEG-encoded digital video. All the programming options of interactive TV that we discuss below require video to be delivered in digital, MPEG format. Interactive TV includes video on demand (you pick the movie, you pick the starting time), interactive game shows (the TV viewers play along in real time), video services (check your bank account balance, pay your bills, shop), and a host of other programming choices. Trials are in progress right now in various parts of the country by telephone and cable companies to assess what viewers want and how to deliver the services. Unfortunately, results of the trials are being kept very secret.

Marriott Hotels has an early presence in this technology, offering video on demand and hotel services via in-room TVs. Video on demand consists of a menu of movie categories with each category accessing a menu of about eight to ten feature movies. Viewers simply tune into one channel to browse the menus, then use the remote control to enter the item number of the movie they wish to see. Movie play begins immediately. Room service, account balances, guest surveys, and checkout are offered on another on-screen menu. All these services are accessed through menu selections via the remote control.

Digital TV companies are offering similar services to home viewers. The service is satellite-based requiring a small (18") satellite dish and a set-top control box. In addition to the standard cable-type channel offerings, feature movies begin every 30 minutes. Priced at about $700 plus a monthly service charge, the system is relatively inexpensive compared to standard satellite dish services.

Many of the titles being developed for CD-based platforms are easily converted for interactive TV, or can be broadcast as is. The CD-i authoring software, MediaMogul, supports the interactive TV format and titles developed with this software can be recorded to disc or compiled for TV and cable networking. The interactive nature of CD-i makes migration to the interactive TV format a natural and easy progression.

THE
PRODUCTION
TEAM

THE PRODUCTION TEAM

The production team for digital video titles develops and supports the project from the idea to the market shelf. Like all publishing, the idea for a project can come from any source, from an artist, application designer, producer, or marketing manager. Once an idea is determined to have merit and to be marketable, the most suitable platform is determined. Then the producer takes over to create "the big picture" and assemble a production team. The production team for digital video titles can be as small as a single person or as large as 10 or 12 specialists. Regardless of the size of the team, there are nine specific disciplines involved in developing digital video titles. The following organizational chart represents one possible structure for the project team.

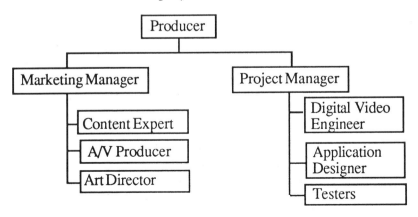

Producer

The digital video producer creates the overall plan and picture of the digital video title. The producer is active in all phases of the process and is responsible for communicating with all team members regarding the purpose, audience, vision, and "look and feel" of the final product. The producer is also responsible for generating the contracts, sub-contracts, financing, hiring, coordination of outside efforts, and scheduling.

Marketing Manager

The marketing manager often oversees the creative side of title production and is directly responsible for determining the title's price, expected demand, audience, distribution strategies, and advertising strategies.

Aspects such as price, expected demand, competitive products, and audience must be determined early in the project life, before the final decision to launch project work and assemble the team. With this information, the project costs can be estimated and compared to project income and decisions about moving forward can be made with the best information at hand.

Distribution and advertising strategies and implementation are late-project tasks. The marketing manager must be able to choose and implement distribution agreements and advertising strategies that will reach the target audience effectively.

The marketing manager should be familiar with market analysis techniques, distribution channels, the CD-ROM or multimedia industry, and target market analysis.

Content Expert

The content expert is responsible for the technical accuracy of the material presented in the title. The content expert determines the scope and logical organization of the information. Typically, the content expert will outline the information required in the title, then work with the application designer to determine the most logical organization for the material. The content expert also writes the original drafts of any scripts, and then reviews and edits final scripts for technical accuracy before audio production begins.

In addition to the obvious technical knowledge that the content expert brings to the project, good communication skills or teaching skills are valuable. CD-ROM or other multimedia is designed very much like good course work and a background in educational principles are very helpful when organizing material for visual presentation.

Audio/Video Producer

The audio/video producer is responsible for the production of the digital video sequences and audio for the project. Production for digital video is fundamentally the same as production for film or video tape, with considerations given to the differences in the delivery of the material. Analog video is delivered to the screen in the form of 30 complete pictures every second. When digitized, a complete video picture is too large in terms of file size to be delivered 30 times per second, so the pictures in the sequence need to be compressed. This compression (more than 200:1) creates some conditions that the video producer needs to allow for when planning and shooting the video. These issues are discussed briefly in the chapter entitled "The Process."

Audio production, likewise, is essentially the same as production for analog delivery. The production involves the same equipment and environment as analog production. Digital sound has been a reality since audio CDs were introduced in 1982, and remains much the same.

The audio/video producer should be educated in digital video planning and production techniques. The producer will need to be familiar with the fundamental title logic in order to plan video transitions between clips.

Art Director/Artist

The art director and/or artist are primarily responsible for the visual flow of information in a digital video title. In projects such as Video CD titles, where there is a great deal of digital video footage, and very few menu or still screens, the artist's job consists of creating an opening screen (bumper) and control screens. In interactive multimedia titles, the artist's job expands to include text-based screens, menus, animations, and transition screens. The digital artist needs to have a good solid background in design elements for a luminescent medium. Color theory for a reflective medium such as paper is very different from luminescent mediums like a TV or computer monitor. Text size and density are critical as is the visual density of background pictures. Elements like on-screen buttons must be carefully designed so that the responses and navigation are intuitive. The placement of interactive elements is critical to the ergonomic success of the title.

Art directors and artists should have a solid background in human factors design, visual rhetoric, and digital art before beginning work in interactive digital media.

Project Manager

The project manager oversees the technical aspects of title production. The project manager defines each stage of the project, sets the project milestones, determines which team members are responsible for each task within the phases, and ensures that each task is completed within the project schedule.

The project manager is primarily a logistician. At the outset of the project, the project manager works closely with each team member defining the scope of work and estimating the time required for each task. Dependencies between team members must be determined. For example, the artist can't begin developing menu screens until the application designer has determined the branching logic. Where dependencies exist, the project manager must juggle the tasks and schedules to make sure that work proceeds as smoothly as possible without team members spending much idle time waiting for other team members to finish.

Project management software is very useful for defining and scheduling projects. Most good software will identify the critical path and show where scheduling conflicts exist. As projects progress, schedule changes that affect dependencies and the critical path are easy to identify. Mac Project Pro from Claris and Microsoft Project are two very good and easy to use project management software packages.

Digital Video Engineer

The digital video engineer is responsible for converting the completed film or tape to the MPEG digital video format. The DV engineer must know how to set up and operate the encoding system, solve problems with the system, and process material for the highest quality encoded video. After video encoding, the DV engineer processes the encoded video and audio files into a single, multiplexed video file that can be included in the application. The digital video engineer should be trained in CD technologies, and have a good understanding of the MPEG specification.

Application Designer/Programmer

The application designer and/or programmer design the program logic for the title. This job varies greatly with the platform chosen. Application designers for interactive multimedia and CD-ROM integrate the audio, video stills, and digital video into a multimedia title. A background in computer programming with a high-level language is helpful, since similar logic skills are needed to develop interactive multimedia. A familiarity with computer-generated art and audio is also very helpful since the application designer will need to be well-versed in the implications of using different picture formats and audio resolutions. For example, some picture formats are digitally very dense and may require several seconds to load and display. When this is necessary, a good application designer will know to start the audio file playing first and use a fade up effect to smooth the transition to the picture.

The application designer should be comfortable with the authoring software used to build the title. Different platforms present different technical issues that affect the production and authoring. Delivery of digital stills or motion video from a CD involves a number of technical issues such as branch times, load times, and seek times that affect how the title plays. A good application designer can use these issues to help the presentation whereas a mediocre or inexperienced application designer will not know how to create smooth transitions or use these delays effectively. Experience with a specific authoring software is not important since the underlying techniques are relatively constant and experience with one authoring tool will easily cross over to other tools.

Programmers are rarely needed when designing digital video titles. The software tools available are designed to make the technology accessible by the creative staff, rather than just the technical staff. The exception is when your title needs special effects not supported by the authoring software. In these cases, you can choose to have the application custom programmed by a staff programmer, or contract a programming group to write a custom subroutine to implement the effect.

Testers

Testers are responsible for testing the final title and ensuring that the title navigation is correct, video and audio are high quality, transitions are smooth, and the interactive elements are both intuitive and functional.

Good testing methodology favors using both an experienced test suite developer and naive users. The test developer uses project documentation to identify what the title is supposed to do, and how errors are handled. The tests are written to exercise all aspects of the title: video, audio, stills, and buttons, as they were designed to be used. An experienced software test engineer is a good choice for this position.

The naive tester is a person who has no familiarity with the title, and represents the consumer. This tester is vital to the market success of the product, and essentially is given the finished title to "play with." The naive tester should personify a typical consumer in terms of industry knowledge, age, and educational background so that the target audience is fairly represented. It's also helpful if this person does not possess above average computer use skills, so the testing can identify icons or buttons that are not intuitive. The naive tester should also be critical and observant and be willing to write down any and all criticisms of the product. It's important that this person not make any assumptions about "this is probably the way the title is supposed to work" and therefore simply report on anything that seems out of place, clumsy, too slow, not easily understood, etc. High school and college students are excellent naive testers and have quality standards that are quite high.

Teamwork

The disciplines involved in the project team are varied and specialized. Groups of this sort tend to contain strong-minded, intelligent, creative people that are both delightful and agonizing to work with. To maximize the delightful and minimize the agony, two characteristics are important: respect and communication. While respect is earned, team leaders can institute an environment that encourages respect for the expertise that each team member brings to the project. Communication must be planned and orchestrated throughout each stage of the project.

In the beginning, careful project planning with the involvement of every team member is the key to a successful project. At the outset of the project, team members need to be familiar with their entire scope of responsibility plus the job descriptions and general responsibilities of the other team members. Distributing the project plans and flowcharts is a good way to formalize the team members' duties.

All team members must have the same vision of the completed project and at the first planning meetings should discuss artistic issues such as the feel and mood of the finished project. This is a good time to familiarize the team with elements like music, color, and mood since these elements will be incorporated in every aspect of design.

During the project, regular project "howgozit" meetings are important to ensuring that all the team members are aware of the progress and stumbling blocks facing the project as a whole. The producer and project manager must trust each team member and be able to communicate the importance of each member's work in the total success of the project. Communication between team members must be encouraged and informal peer reviews of the various elements can be a great help in keeping the project elements cohesive.

After the project is completed and in distribution, a wrap-up meeting is especially helpful. After the celebrating, the entire team has a chance to reflect on the project and discuss what went well and why, and what went wrong and why. One of the attendees should take notes and then distribute the "what we learned" paper to all team members to reinforce the meeting. Learning from past projects is the most valuable experience any team member can bring to the next project and post-project meetings give the team the opportunity to formalize the lessons learned.

THE
DIGITAL
VIDEO
STUDIO

THE DIGITAL VIDEO STUDIO

The digital video studio consists of audio/visual equipment, computer hardware, and computer software. Like any successful production facility, the studio must be equipped with the highest quality hardware and software so that the highest quality title can be produced. In this chapter, we'll discuss the equipment and software needed to outfit a complete production studio.

Not every digital video or multimedia production company needs a fully equipped studio. Service bureaus can be employed to encode video and create digital video files, so a production company may be fully operational with less equipment and the phone number of a good service bureau. The resource guide at the end of this book gives a listing of companies that specialize in particular areas of title production.

Regardless of the complexity or sophistication of the studio, every person producing a digital video or multimedia title should be familiar with the process and the equipment that goes into the process.

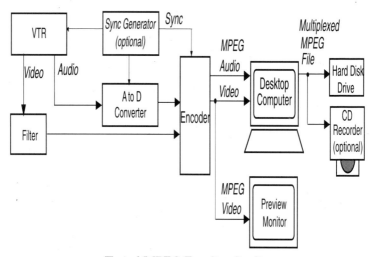

Typical MPEG Encoding Studio

After the source film or video is produced and edited, it is taken on video to the MPEG studio so it can be encoded. This is in the last stages of video production. The MPEG encoding studio provides the hardware and software equipment to take the produced tape and convert it to digital video. The encoded video clips can then be authored into multimedia titles, Video CDs, and interactive TV titles. The authoring process involves selecting programming commands to combine the digital video, digital audio, and still images into a cohesive, working project.

A good encoding system will process the source video in "real-time." This means that 30 minutes of source tape will take 30 minutes to encode. The actual lag between the input video and output file is less than two seconds. The newly encoded video can be viewed during the encoding process if you use the optional preview monitor. Without the preview monitor, the encoded file can be played back immediately following encoding. Some of the better encoding systems allow you to display the source tape and encoded video side-by-side on the preview monitor during encoding. This feature is especially nice for comparing quality, and identifying specific problem areas in the video clip. Although no editing of the video can take place during or after encoding, you can make adjustments to the video filter or video noise reduction unit during encoding to boost the picture quality of the encoded video.

The video engineer at the Electric Switch, Ltd. MPEG encoding studio has video controls and tape deck mounted in a control panel, and two monitors mounted in the facing wall. The Macintosh, at the right, controls the encoding software.

Photograph © 1995 Electric Switch, Ltd. Used by permission

A/V Equipment

Betacam or D1 Camera

Either of these cameras offers the high-quality video that encoding requires. The Betacam output is analog, and the D1 is digital.

Many digital video producers prefer to shoot the source video on film, then transfer the film to one of the above tapes. Producing film first provides the best quality when the footage needs editing or enhancing. After the post production work, the film can then be transferred to a tape for encoding.

Betacam or D1 VTR

Which one you choose is largely a matter of preference and availability. Some encoding software provides on-screen VTR control; if not, a separate VTR control box will be needed.

Sync Generator

A sync generator provides a video sync signal to the VTR, A to D converter, encoding hardware, and computer. This is optional since an adequate sync signal can be supplied by the encoding hardware.

Filter

The filter lets you adjust and filter the source video while encoding.

Analog to Digital Converter

If you are using Betacam source tape, the analog to digital converter pre-converts your source into a digital format before encoding.

The MPEG encoding studio at Electric Switch, Ltd. is equipped with a Macintosh-based encoding system and dual-preview monitors. One of the monitors displays the source tape, and one of the monitors displays the encoded video. With the two monitors, you can evaluate the quality of the encoded video and make adjustments in filtering, to keep your encoded video as close to source quality as possible.

Photograph © 1995, Electric Switch, Ltd. Used by permission

Video Preview Monitor

The preview monitor displays the encoded video directly after encoding so that you can monitor the quality of the encoded video in progress. The better encoding systems allow you to view a split screen with source and encoded video displayed side by side.

Audio Recording and Mixing

Audio recording and mixing does not differ from standard audio production. All audio dubbing and mixing takes place during the source video editing or post-production phase. The encoding systems provide little to no

49

control over audio so all audio work must be complete before encoding. However, completed, separate tracks can be encoded, for instance for foreign language editions.

Computer Hardware

High-End Personal Computer
A Macintosh Quadra, 486 or Pentium-based PC, or Sun Sparc workstation is needed to keep up with the heavy demands of the encoding.

High-Capacity Disk Drive
Initially, the encoded video and audio are stored in files on a computer hard drive. A capacity of 2 Gigabyte or more is recommended.

Encoding System Extension or Encoder Board
Most encoding systems require separate housing for the encoder hardware. This extension should be included with the encoding system package, with the cables required to connect to other equipment.

Note: Software-only MPEG encoders are available from many sources, including some that are distributed electronically as shareware. Those encoding systems are not discussed here as a studio option. Be aware that the software-only encoding systems are not professional quality. The encoding process with these systems typically takes 60 hours or more for 1 hour of video, and the quality is low and difficult to control. The software-only encoders may be a viable option for digital video producers that use very few, very short video clips, or where quality is not of great concern.

The digital video encoder is housed in a separate chassis that connects to a desktop computer. The Delta Vx encoder shown here contains four cards: video capture card, audio capture card, encoder card, and decoder card. It connects to a Macintosh through a fiber optic cable.

Photographs © 1995, OptImage Interactive Services

CD Recorder

(Recommended) A CD recorder connects to your personal computer and records Write Once compact discs. This hardware is not strictly required, but if your title will be distributed on compact disc, such as Video CD, CD-i, or CD-ROM, you'll benefit by testing your finished title in the most accurate environment possible. The Write Once CD can also be shipped to the disc replication facility for mass production.

An alternative to a CD recorder is an emulator. Emulators are available for Video CD and CD-i titles, but are not necessary of available, for CD-ROM. Emulators mimic the characteristics of the players and allow you to do very precise testing from a disc image, before committing your title to a CD. The disc image can then be recorded to a tape and sent to a disc replication facility. Since emulators aren't available for CD-ROM, the most accurate method of testing these applications are from the Write Once CD.

Consumer Players

When your title is finished, you'll need to test it on all the different consumer players on which the title is designed to play. You'll also need to test the title on NTSC and PAL monitors if the title will sell in both the US and Europe. CD-ROM titles should be thoroughly tested on the minimum possible computer configuration to ensure that screen sizes and color choices work with small screens and monitors that display fewer colors.

Computer Software

Graphics Design Software

For creating the still images and control panels, you'll need drawing and paint graphics software. Any good, professional-quality graphics packages can be used. Additionally, you'll need plug-ins or specialized conversion software that allows you to export the finished images to the special formats required by Video CD and/or CD-i. Your authoring system vendor can help you identify which conversion packages work best with your favorite graphics programs.

Audio Conversion Software

If you are planning to include audio files that are separate from the MPEG tape source, you'll need to capture and digitize audio files. Sound Designer is a good package that is widely supported, and your authoring system vendor can identify others that will work well with your system.

MPEG Encoding Software

Encoding software minimally consists of VTR control, encoding control software, and multiplexing software. The final result of the encoding software should be multiplexed MPEG A/V streams and entry point lists.

Authoring System with Digital Video Capabilities

The authoring system depends on the platform you are targeting. It must be capable of supporting MPEG digital video files within the application. Authoring systems may require additional hardware, or additional graphics and audio software.

The authoring system provides the format where you assemble your still audio/video and motion audio/video together with instructions that specify what to display at what times, how the user controls the application, and what choices the user can make at specific times.

Mastering Software

After a title is authored, a disc image may have to be mastered before the title can be pressed on a disc. The mastering software "compiles" the application by arranging files, optimizing the data, and preparing the low-level CD physical requirements. The requirement for mastering software varies with the authoring software and platform.

CD Recording Software

CD recording software allows you to connect a CD recorder to your computer and record a master disc. The process is fairly straightforward, but some software is much easier to use than others. The best CD recording software packages support a large number of disc formats and are useful with many platforms. The resulting master disc can be used for final testing and sent to a disc replication facility for mass production.

THE
PROCESS

THE PROCESS

The digital video project can be defined in a specific sequence of events that lead you from concept to finished product. By adopting a formal process, you will save time and money, while avoiding some huge frustrations. You'll be comfortable knowing that all of your team members are working with the same vision and that potential problems have been identified and dealt with before they occur. The project can be broken down into five phases. Each phase has a number of associated tasks and a specific result. In a contracted project, the result of each phase can be a contracted deliverable item. In an internal project, the result of each phase can be tested against the specifications before proceeding with the next project phase.

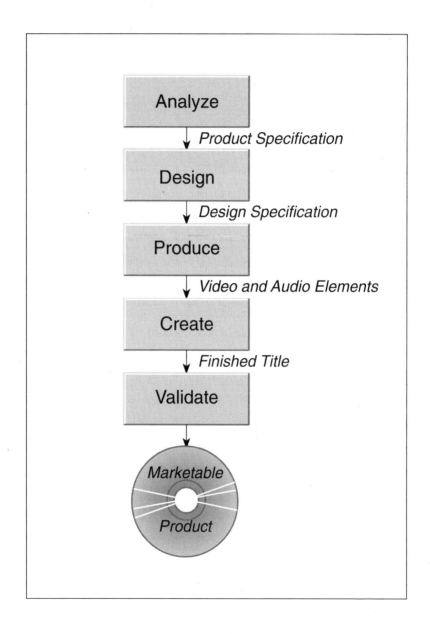

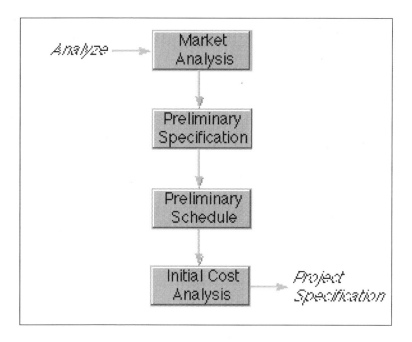

Analyze

The analysis phase of the multimedia or digital video project answers the question, "Is this really a good idea?" By breaking that question down into several specific and quantifiable tests or questions, you'll know to a fairly high degree of accuracy if the project is marketable, possible, financially feasible, timely, and profitable. The analysis phase consists of four primary tasks. You should expect to spend about 25% of your total project time on the analysis phase. The result of the analysis phase is a complete and thoughtful project specification.

Analysis

A market analysis explores the marketing issues involved in the project. Each of the following issues should be decided on and become a section of the project specification:

- **Purpose**

A description of the fundamental reason why the product is being developed.

- **Target Audience**

Basic demographics of the audience who will buy the product including age, income group, and educational level. The demographic profile might also include a description of the special skills and equipment needs of the target audience.

- **Platform**

From the demographic profile and stated purpose, you can usually narrow down platform choices easily and quickly. Some platforms are simply better suited for certain designs than others or the availability of the platform to the target audience may be the determining factor.

- **Target Price**

The target price for any product is simply "what the market will bear" and will depend mostly on the price of similar or competing products.

- **Competing Products**

By closely examining the competition you can not only estimate the target price, you can also discover how your product can function better, faster, more ergonomically, more logically, and have greater perceived value and quality. If there are no competing products, why do no similar products exist? Competing products can also provide a good insight into the product demand.

- **Distribution Channels**

Which distribution channels will give you the greatest exposure to your target audience? Your demographic profile may also include an analysis of where your target audience shops.

Preliminary Specification
The preliminary specification is the first draft of a document that will evolve over the life of the product. This document serves as the primary communication with all project members and defines the project in fairly specific but high-level terms. This is where hundreds of details are set down on paper, defining both the product and the project. The preliminary specification consists of two major parts: the marketing specification and the design specification.

The marketing specification section builds on the market analysis to determine target audience, target price, expected demand, and marketing strategies. The purpose of the product should be clearly and specifically stated in the marketing specification. Together with these details, the marketing specification provides a general view of the product from the user's standpoint. It defines the artistic style, color, and audio style. Depending on the autonomy that each of the team members have, the specification can be quite esoteric or quite specific. The marketing specification also provides the level of interactivity of the product as well as its functional description.

The design specification section deals with the more technical aspects of the project. The design spec includes information about the equipment and software required for the project, human resource estimates, outsource resources, preliminary flowcharts, and language or authoring tool specifications. The fundamental design of the product is described in this section in terms understandable by both the marketing and product design team members.

The preliminary specification is critical to the success of the project. Once written, it becomes the foundation for project work that ensures all the team members are working along the same track. The preliminary specification should be available to all team members for discussion and input, and finally for reference.

Over the life of the project, the preliminary specification should be reviewed periodically and modified to address changes. These reviews and re-writes should be planned at specific stages of the project and the resulting amended document can be distributed to team members. Be sure to keep every revision of the specification so that you have an historical record of your project.

Preliminary Schedule

The preliminary schedule shows the life cycle of the project in terms of time estimates, resource loading, and critical path. Basic project management software or manually prepared PERT or GANTT charts provide an easily visible overview of the project so that delays or spec changes can be quickly evaluated for their impact on the total project.

Project management software automatically defines the critical path of the project. Since several tasks are almost always going on simultaneously, identifying the critical path makes it easy to determine where a delay may affect the project release dates.

The preliminary schedule can be added to the preliminary specification as an appendix.

Initial Cost Analysis

The second appendix to the preliminary specification should be the initial cost analysis. This analysis includes personnel costs, special equipment costs, general equipment depreciation, software costs or depreciation, contract fees, packaging costs, advertising costs, and business overhead.

When the cost analysis is completed, it can be compared to the target price and estimated sales to determine at what point the expenses will be paid and profits can be made. With this analysis, you can develop a realistic budget and make an intelligent and informed decision about whether to proceed, if and where to reduce costs, and if and what adjustments to make in the marketing plan.

Design

After you have developed your "big picture" vision of your project, it's time to start working on the details. The project design develops from the preliminary specification to create a design specification. The design specification may take one or more different forms. It may look like a specification document, a flowchart, a collection of storyboards, or most likely, a combination of different forms. The design specification details the program logic, modularity, and cross-platform specifications.

Storyboards

Storyboards are a visual representation of the title flow. Storyboards use a type of simple flowchart logic, but usually consist of pictures or draft drawings that represent the visual aspects of the title. Developing storyboards is helpful for fast prototyping of a project and can identify design and logic problems, or where special logic needs to be developed. Another method of prototyping is the use of electronic prototyping tools. Tools such as Claris HyperCard or Asymetrix Toolbook can give you a fast electronic prototype of your title, and allow you to build simple segments of your title for testing.

Flowcharts

Flowcharts graphically display the program logic. Flowcharts can be very simple boxes and arrows, or more complex with decision trees and modules identified. When the multimedia project is quite simple like a linear movie title, a flowchart may not even be worth the time it takes to create. For more complex multimedia titles, a flowchart can prevent a lot of frustration and help keep track of branches, returns, and variables. It always helps, though, to decide early on what symbols you will use in your flowcharts and what level of detail is appropriate and helpful.

A single, simple flowchart that displays the entire program logic should be part of each team member's reference package. Beyond that, a specific flowchart for each team member involved in the production work may be very helpful. For instance, a flowchart for the graphic artist will detail where menu screens or still video screens are required and what relationships exist between screens. With this information, the artist can produce sequences of screens that are visually logical and cohesive.

The multimedia author will require flowcharts that are much more complex than required by most team members. These flowcharts describe in detail the menus, screens, branches, returns, variables, and navigation at each module of the application.

Modularity
When planning your project, don't forget to plan for modular testing. Each of the production tasks can be tested separately, and titles can be tested in modules during title scripting.

When the various elements of the title have been developed, have the other team members review and test the completed elements. Have the video producer review the still video screens and menus, the artist review the audio files, the application designer review the motion video, and the project manager review everything.

Peer testing and reviews are also valuable from sources outside the immediate project. A video engineer and/or producer can offer critical and valuable insight to the motion video production. A graphic artist can provide specific advice about video stills and menus. A content expert can identify weaknesses in the presentation of the material and inaccuracies that can sneak in.

Modular testing is extremely important in terms of the total project. Errors are cheap and easy to fix during production, and expensive and difficult to fix if they are discovered at the end of the process.

Cross-Platform Considerations
When planning and specifying a multimedia digital video title, you may want to consider authoring your title for more than one platform. With CD-ROM titles, you can market to over 90% of the CD-ROM market by building your title to play on both Macintosh and PC (DOS) platforms. A Video CD title can be authored for Video CD and CD-i easily, and can also be authored for the CD-ROM market at the same time.

The easiest MPEG platform to author cross-platform applications for is Video CD. The Video CD spec allows you to include control applications for other platforms in track 1 of the CD. In some cases, a control application is not needed if the MPEG playback board contains the control application in firmware. Video CDs contain no Video CD control application since the Video CD player controls playback through the hardware, much like audio CD players. When a Video CD that is authored for several platforms is played, the platform playing the title recognizes only the "native" control application, and ignores the others, or uses the control application that is in the MPEG board firmware. The following illustration shows a Video CD application authored for four platforms. Each of the application files contains the play and control instructions for that specific platform. All applications access the same set of MPEG digital video files. A CD-i player will only recognize the CD-i application; the others are ignored.

Macintosh/PC digital video CD-ROM is another easy combination. A special disk format, called a Hybrid disc, is allowed by several CD recording software packages. A hybrid disc contains both PC and Macintosh file structures and the better disc recording packages allow you to share data files between the two structures, like in the illustration that follows. Using a recording software that allows you to share the data files is a much better choice.

Since you don't have to include two sets of the data files, you can nearly double the amount of information the disc will store.

Remember though, with each new platform you add, you complicate the process and introduce a new possible source of incompatibility and error. Take your time to investigate the details. Disc Manufacturing, Inc. (DMI) published a very good technical manual on architecture. It's listed in the recommended reading section with information on how to contact DMI.

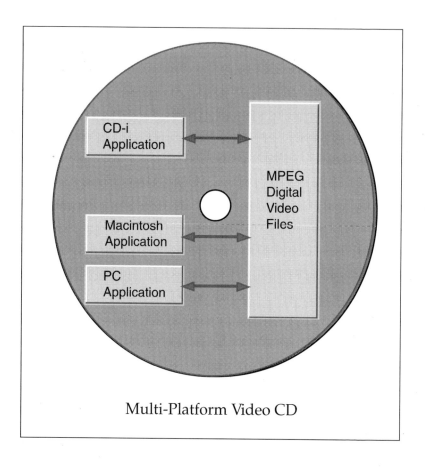

Multi-Platform Video CD

Produce

The production phase involves several tasks that can be accomplished simultaneously. Motion video production, still video production, and audio production can be in process at the same time with different teams.

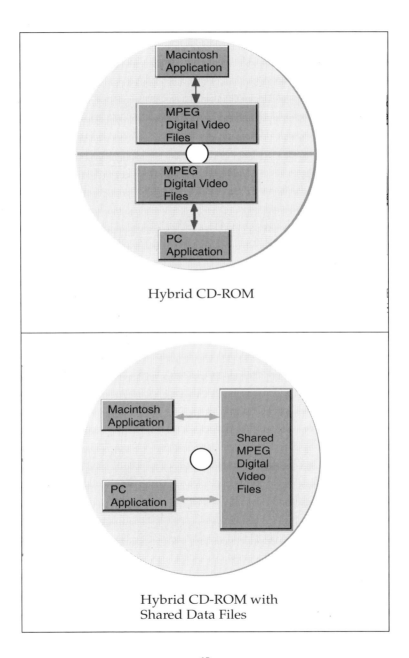

Hybrid CD-ROM

Hybrid CD-ROM with
Shared Data Files

Digital Video Production

Before beginning production, consider the following questions:

1. What type of TV set will connect to the player?

NTSC sets deliver video to the screen at 30 frames per second and have a screen size of 352 X 240 pixels.

PAL sets deliver video to the screen at 25 frames per second and have a screen size of 352 X 288 pixels.

When an NTSC video is viewed on a PAL television set, the video will contain a narrow black margin at the top and bottom of the screen. When a PAL video is viewed on an NTSC set, a narrow strip of video at the top and bottom of the screen will be lost. There will also be some compromise in pixel aspect ratio, but this is generally not a problem.

If you are producing a title that will play on both sets, the rule of thumb to remember is: Record and encode the video in PAL format, but keep all critical visual information within the "safe" area for NTSC. This is a 320 X 210 pixel square centered in the screen.

MPEG decoders adjust automatically for the difference in delivery rates between PAL (25 frames per second) and NTSC (30 frames per second).

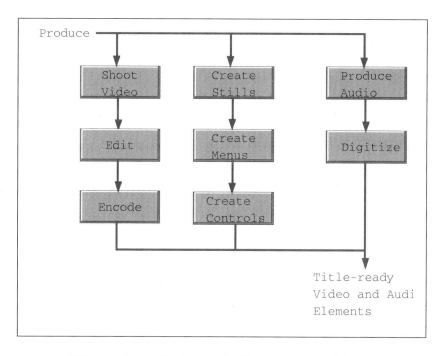

2. What other platforms will play this title?

If you are creating a title that will play on more than one platform, plan your video production to play on the most restricted platform. For instance, Video CD requires a narrower screen and more restrictive data delivery rates than the other digital video platforms. For a title to play on a Video CD player as well as other platforms, it must conform to the tightest of the specifications. The most restrictive specification must be the specification that governs your production to guarantee your title will play on all intended platforms.

71

3. What formats does your encoding system allow?

PAL source must be encoded on a PAL encoding system. NTSC source must be encoded on an NTSC encoding system. You cannot mix the two formats successfully when encoding. The better encoding systems will configure to either standard.

Video Quality

Video quality is an important issue with digital video. Because the encoded video is compressed about 225 times, there is a great deal of video information that is "lost" in the process of encoding. The encoding process is an intelligent process, and the encoding system is designed to optimize both video and audio. With some particular production work and techniques, quality of the video does not need to display any discernible loss. Digital video encoded to the MPEG1 standard is advertised as being "VHS-quality video." VHS quality is the lowest quality that you can expect with MPEG1 digital video, and many producers are achieving very close to broadcast-quality video with MPEG1.

Video quality is most often related to the visual density of the footage. When the encoder must create a series of frames that are rapidly changing, the density of the information may be too high and cause some ugly visual artifacts in the encoded video such as blank horizontal or vertical lines.

All the rules of good classic video and film production apply as well in digital video production, but even more critically. A black and white hounds tooth jacket is irritating in standard production. In digital video production, it can make a scene impossible to encode.

Following are some general guidelines to remember during production and encoding:

- **Backgrounds**

Backgrounds that are static or slowly changing are easier to encode than backgrounds that are quite dynamic. For example, if you are shooting a scene of dolphins moving through water, you can shoot the scene under water or above the water. Under water the background is more sedate. There is little glare from the sun, and the colors of the background have less contrast. Above water, the surface of the water contains more glare, more contrasting colors, and sharper definition. Encoding the scene filmed above the water will be more difficult than below water and demand a higher level of filtering.

Shooting fire and explosions can create other troublesome scenes. Both of these scenes are changing very rapidly visually, and the more of the screen that the fire or explosion occupies, the more chance you will have jerky, choppy encoded video.

High-contrast diagonal lines such as a room with miniblinds, can look shimmery and distracting when encoded. In general, try to avoid high contrast stripes.

- **Transition Effects**

Avoid dissolves. Any transition effect that requires massive pixel changes from frame to frame will be troublesome when encoding. Dissolves can work in circumstances where you dissolve to a very similar frame, such as when a person appears or disappears on the screen.

Avoid fade up from black or fade down to black. Like dissolves, these effects require that a large percentage of the screen pixels change all at once.

Wipes, curtains, horizontal or vertical blinds, and mosaic effects all encode quite easily.

Filtering and Encoding

After producing the video sequences, you are ready to encode. If you produced your video on film, first transfer the film to high-quality source tape. The encoding process involves pre-processing (filtering), analog-to-digital conversion, encoding, and multiplexing.

The video output of the VTR deck can be directly input to a video filter. As well as reducing the video noise, the filter allows you to make fine adjustments in picture quality to make the video cleaner and easier to encode. The better encoding systems allow you to preview the encoded video alongside the source video on the same monitor. With the two videos side by side, you can objectively view the differences between the two, and adjust the filtering to minimize the difference.

When dealing with difficult video footage, start by limiting the dynamic range of the video. Raise the black level, lower the white level, diminish the chroma slightly, and limit the bandwidth to between 3 and 4 MHz. You can use an anti-aliasing (smoothing) filter to soften sharp edges.

Analog-to-digital conversion is only necessary if you are using analog source tape. This is accomplished with a simple video-in, video-out converter box. There are no variables or adjustments, simply connect the A to D converter between the output of the VTR and the input of the encoding system.

Once the hardware connections have been made, encoding is fairly simple and automatic. The encoding software allows you to define the output file name and define entry points. Entry points are frames in the digital video stream that are complete pictures and allow viewers to jump into the video. The encoding software automatically builds a complete picture frame at regular intervals such as every 1/2 second, or when the picture has changed dramatically, but an entry point list gives you

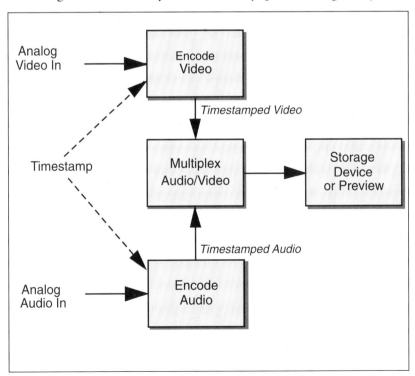

more control over the process and precisely defines where you want to be able to enter the video.

When the video has been encoded, you have two digital files: an audio file and a video file. Both files contain timing information. After encoding, the next step is multiplexing. This may be a separate process, or may be accomplished automatically by the encoding software. Multiplexing involves joining the audio and video into a single digital file. The timing information in each file guarantees the synchronization of audio and video. The final product of multiplexing is the MPEG files that you can combine with the still video elements to create your application.

Video Stills and Controls
When producing digital video for CD-i or CD-ROM multimedia, you'll need to plan and produce the menu screens that contain the program controls. Video CD also allows still images and menu screens in the work. If your project is a linear video, you'll need a title screen or bumper, menu screens, and a control panel screen. The title screen most often is a short animation with audio very much like the production company logo presented at the beginning of any feature film.

Still video and animation can be created using many existing Macintosh or PC drawing and painting tools. Any tool that can produce IFF, Targa, Vista, GIF, PCX, LBM, PICT, or PICT2 files can be used. After the files are created, they must be converted to the resolutions required by the target platform. It's also a very good idea to preview the files on the target platform to make sure that the color combinations look good and the text is legible.

A menu screen offers the viewers a way of jumping ahead in a movie without needing to scan. Typical menu screens are similar to a table of contents in a book, or a general outline of the movie. Each line in the screen is actually a button that the viewer can select to jump to that "chapter." Linear movies require two discs to hold the full content. For these, there are usually two menu screens, one on each disc. Both menus contain the entire table of contents, indicating which chapters are located on the other disc.

Multimedia titles may contain many menu screens, representing many levels of play. Menus can take many different forms. Some examples of menu design are: A view of a room with doors leading to different application areas, a picture of a town with different buildings leading to different areas, a set of icons pictorially representing different selections, and the more traditional buttons that activate different selections. In every case, the user either moves an on-screen cursor, slides a mouse or control up or down to highlight, or selects a number to branch the application to a specific area. The design of the menu screens must be intuitive enough that the user knows the purpose of the screen and can navigate without confusion. Some multimedia titles make use of a "map" that is available from anywhere in the application. The map is accessed from a hotspot and small icon that appear on every menu and many screens. This map displays the application structure in such a way that the user can jump quickly to any level without being forced to follow a structured and sometimes convoluted path through the application.

Digital video controls are very similar to a VCR control panel. When on-screen controls are required to be a part of the application as they are for CD-i, they are usually hidden. The viewer simply presses a button on the remote control, and the control panel pops up from the bottom of the screen. A typical on-screen control panel such as the one pictured below will have buttons for forward and reverse scan, slow motion, pause, continue, menu, mute, freeze, normal, and stop, as well as volume controls.

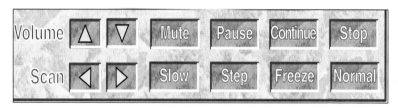

On-Screen Control Panel

Colors, Buttons, Design Elements

Multimedia screen design integrates elements of art, visual rhetoric, and human factors engineering. Information must be presented in a lively entertaining way to keep the viewer's interest, must present the correct amount of information on each screen, and must present information in a logical and comprehensible fashion. Text elements, such as titles, must be easily readable from an average distance of 8 to 10 feet.

Screen design can be judged against the traditional six elements of visual design.

- **Figure-Ground Segregation**
Primarily involves size and contrast and the ability to easily distinguish elements from the background.

- **Symmetry**
Overall balance of the screen design.

- **Proximity**
Related elements are organized close to each other.

- **Closure**
Related concepts are grouped visually and distanced from unrelated concepts.

- **Continuation**
Information visually flows beyond the termination of the screen.

- **Similarity**
Related groups of information resemble each other visually. When the visual elements change, there is also a change in content or subject.

Use of color is a bit more complicated. While color plays a large role in the six basic design elements and can be used very effectively to provide closure and continuation, there are psychological effects of color that need to be taken into account. The choice of hue, saturation, and intensity should be carefully chosen to match the basic design, audience, and mood of the title.

Audio Elements

Audio elements, other than the digital video audio, can be recorded on a PC or Macintosh using a good quality sound capture and editing package. All audio elements can be formatted for the target platform, or can be converted to MPEG audio formats for cross-platform use.

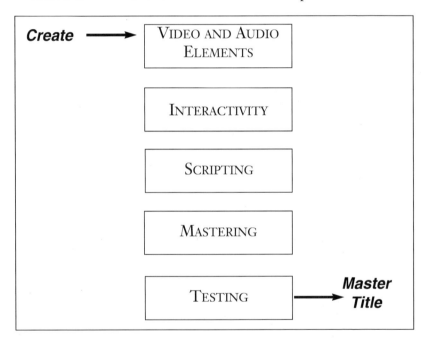

Create

The creation, or authoring, process combines all of the screen images, digital video, and audio into a single cohesive working title by integrating them with programming commands. The authoring process varies from platform to platform and title to title. Authoring a simple, linear, Video CD title can be as easy as writing a "script," a simple list of commands, that names the digital video file and the CD-i application file.

Interactivity
Video CD titles allow a small degree of interactivity. While this format is most like video tape, a menu screen is displayable at any time during play. A typical menu screen works very much like a book's Table of Contents and lets the viewers jump to various parts of the work. In the case of a catalog-style presentation, the menu will list all the short clips that are available. Viewers can select "chapters" from the menu and jump directly to any chapter or clip by selecting a menu item.

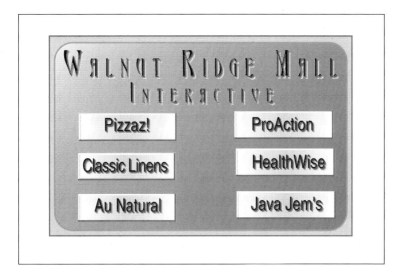

Interactive multimedia titles are created with authoring tools (software) that provide an easy to use interface to

develop the timing, branching, and other interactive elements. An interactive title is composed of "scripts" that you generate within the authoring tool. A script is a set of instructions, similar to but simpler than a computer program. A separate script is generated for each linear portion of a title. A script ends with a set of branches to other scripts, or a return to a previous script, or the end of the title.

The level of interactivity in multimedia titles can be quite complex and involve thousands of individual scripts and levels. The main menu in an interactive multimedia title will often lead to other, more specific menus which, in turn, lead to scripts containing even more menus.

Creating a flowchart as part of the project specification provides an easy to use map of the interactivity, and can be as simple or intricate as your team and project requires. The flowchart also provides the first visual test of the project — it's an easy way to make sure that the title doesn't dead end or lead to endless, inescapable loops.

Scripting
The scripting of a digital video title involves identifying the logical flow of the title. Opening bumper... to menu... to video clips... to menu... and so on. Different authoring tools provide different paradigms to the scripting process, although all provide essentially the same output. Your choice of which authoring tool to use should be based on the capabilities of the authoring tool, especially the digital video capabilities.

• Timeline Scripting

One paradigm is the timeline. Timeline-based scripting tools provide a spreadsheet interface on which you enter time, video elements, audio elements, program commands, and video effects. The following illustration shows a sample script from the MediaMogul authoring tool for interactive TV and CD-i.

This is the opening script of a CD-i application developed with MediaMogul. This application is a multistore catalog for a strip mall, and it allows viewers to browse different stores, check merchandise, pricing, payment terms, and delivery schedules. Digital video clips are used to demonstrate merchandise.

START	00:00	03:00	10:00	
DURATION	03:00	09:00		
FILE	logo.cl	bumper.anm	mall.cl	
EFFECT	Fade Up	Animate 15	Curtain	
INSET				
DURATION	02:00		00:15	
FILE	bumper.b			
EFFECT	Play			
INSET				
DURATION	12:00			
FILE			mall.m	
CONTROL			Wait	
VARIABLE				
VALUE				

Timeline Script

83

Column 1: The script starts with a 2 second fade up effect to a still video file (logo.cl) and begins play of a 12 second audio file (bumper. b). After the fade up, the still video holds on the screen for an additional 1 second for a total duration of 3 seconds.

Column 2: The audio file continues to play and an 8 second animated corporate bumper (bumper.anm) is played. The last frame of the bumper holds for one second. Since the first frame of the animation is identical to the still video displayed in the opening, there is no visible transition from the opening screen to the animation file.

Column 3: A curtain close effect that lasts for a half second (15 frames) displays a video file that is a wide-angle view of a strip mall. Each storefront in the picture is a button, and a cursor appears on the screen. As the cursor passes over a storefront, its color changes. This video file is actually a menu file that branches to a number of different scripts. This screen remains displayed until the viewer makes a choice of which store to enter, then a branch is executed.

In this authoring tool, the menu screens actually consist of two files. One file is a still video image. The second file is the actual menu file. The menu file is created as an overlay to the still video image and is completely transparent. Creating a menu file involves displaying the still image file and drawing "hotspots" around each of the shapes that will be selection buttons. When the hotspot is drawn, you define which script will be branched to the button. This process keeps scripting simple so that a single script column can branch to a large number of scripts with a single branch command such as "wait," as shown in column 3. When a viewer makes a choice from the menu, the script then branches to another script for the specific shop selected. Next the viewer can choose from merchandise or departments, and view the digital video clips that demonstrate the merchandise.

- **Video CD scripting**

Video CD titles are among the easiest to script. The Video CD Toolkit authoring software provides simple windows from which to specify the elements that make up a Video CD title, then builds the disc image when you click the *OK* button.

A Video CD title consists of an album, which is the entire application, and volumes, which are individual CDs. This structure allows you to break your title across more than one CD. In addition to the MPEG digital video files, a Video CD can also contain a copyright file, abstract file, and bibliography file. These are all text files that you can create, or you can use the files that are included with the authoring tool. The process then continues as you create a list of MPEG files to include from a browser window. After selecting the MPEG files, the software builds the disc image.

- **Mastering**

When scripting is complete, titles often need to be mastered. The need for mastering depends on the platform and authoring tool. The process of mastering is very similar to compilation of a computer program. Before a disc can be pressed or played on an interactive TV network, the files are assembled and compressed into a single application file.

While the actual mastering process is extremely complex, the complexity is internal to the mastering program and it is quite simple for the project author. In its simplest form, mastering consists of selecting the starting script of the application or selecting the Video CD album file. Then you simply click the *OK* button to begin mastering. The mastering software then starts to work, reading the script, collecting the associated scripts, audio files, still images, and digital video files, creating a single file that contains all the application elements, and organizing all the elements for the best access times from a disc.

Validate

After the title has been mastered, the complete application must be validated. Validation testing of the mastered application is critical because data delivered from a CD involves timing considerations that can't be accurately represented on the authoring system. Branch times, seek times, and audio synchronization (other than digital video) may be quite different from the authoring system to the CD. For testing purposes, the title can be either emulated, or a check disc can be recorded and tested on an actual player or CD-ROM drive.

Emulating Video CD and CD-i involves the use of a separate piece of hardware called an emulator. An emulator perfectly mimics a CD-i player and lets you test your title before pressing a disc. The emulator connects to your authoring system, reads the disc image, and delivers the title to a monitor in exactly the same way a CD delivers data. If adjustments need to be made, you can edit the scripts and re-master the disc image.

When testing is complete and you have a final working disc image, you can either record a write-once disc, or send the image file to a replication service company to have the final product replicated.

Check Discs for All Platforms

Creating check discs requires that you have a compact disc recorder and recording software. This relatively simple process involves connecting the disc recorder, selecting the disc image file, loading a blank disc, then letting the software take over to burn a check disc. You'll need to create a separate check disc for each platform that you'll be distributing.

Platform Testing

After the disc is recorded, the check disc can be tested in the target platform or platforms. For cross-platform titles, it is especially important to test in all the different platforms that will play the disc.

If you are testing a CD-ROM application, be sure to test your title in several different CD-ROM drives. CD-ROM drives are available in different speeds. Your application will behave slightly differently in a 1X, 2X, or 4X drive.

Logic Testing

In this test, you give the title to one or more testers who are representative of the target audience. Their job is to simply play the title, make selections, and watch for flawed logic, logical dead ends, menu screens or control panels that aren't clear and simple, and video flaws. Good logic testing will use testers who offer different expertise. High school students are quite good testers and typically have very high expectations. A video engineer or producer can accurately judge the video quality and offer valuable comments about the video production. Content experts outside of the project team can test for content accuracy and logical flow of information.

Timing Testing

Because the authoring environment does not accurately represent the timing of an application delivered from a CD, you need to set aside a separate block of testing time to check the branch and seek times of your finished title. If you find branch and seek times that are clumsy or distracting, you can adjust your title to compensate for these flaws.

Adjustments can be made to the application scripts and new check discs can be recorded until the title works perfectly. The final disc can then be sent to a replication facility.

Your choice of whether you will emulate the disc image or record a write-once disc for testing depends largely on how you plan to distribute your title. If you will be producing hundreds or thousands of copies of the title, you may decide to use an emulator and not produce check discs. If you will be producing just a few (less than 100) discs of each title, you may choose to do all of your disc replication in house. If this is so, recording check discs makes sense. Likewise, some platforms such as CD-ROM do not have available emulators, and recording check discs may be your only choice.

LAUNCHING YOUR TITLE

LAUNCHING YOUR TITLE

Now that you have a finished title, you can turn your attention to the marketplace and work can shift to packaging, disc artwork, legal issues, product manufacturing, and distribution.

Product Packaging

Disc Artwork

If your title is delivered on a CD, the top of the CD can be screened by the disc replication facility with artwork. This artwork should include a copyright notice (© *year, company name*). Disc artwork is specified in terms of size, image area, and number of colors by the disc replication facility, and is delivered on film with the master disc.

Packaging

There are a number of options available for packaging a CD. You can choose from the traditional jewel case with an insert, a plastic sleeve with a paper insert, a ringbinder sleeve that can be included in the package with your documentation, or even your own CD packaging design.

If your product has more pieces than just a CD, you'll need to design product packaging that assembles all the pieces into a single package. Mailing packages may also be needed depending on your choice of distribution.

Copyrights

Copyright law is complex and your product deserves the attention of a good attorney specializing in copyrights and trademarks. All published work is copyrighted on first publication. This is true even if you choose not to register your copyright. This type of copyright, however, carries with it a limited set of rights. To have access to the full weight of copyright law, you must register your work with the copyright office.

Registering your work involves sending a copy of the finished work with paper copies of the authoring or scripts to the copyright office with a Form T. When you register the finished work, you automatically register all original screen artwork and audio included in the title, so there is usually no need to register the individual elements of your title separately.

If your title includes custom computer code, you may also need to register the code separately from the program, particularly if that code implements new functions or can be classified as company proprietary or trade secret. Again, a copyright and trademarks attorney can help you understand the law and process.

Duplication

Disc duplication (replication) services receive your master disc, artwork, and packaging requirements, and mass produce the CDs. This process takes from 5 to 15 days after receipt of the master disc, and prices for the service vary depending on turn-around time, quantity, and packaging. When you are in the final stages of product development, call the replication facility and discuss schedules, numbers, packaging, etc. with an account representative. Check the resources section of this book for a listing of the major disc replication companies.

Distribution

Now that your project is all dressed up and ready to face the world, it's time to think about distribution and advertising. Distribution channels for Video CD and multimedia vary widely depending on content and target audience.

For professional education and training titles, professional organizations sometimes offer referral services to preferred vendors. Likewise, vendor listings for major trade shows will provide some good leads to vendors that have a similar target audience. Professional trade magazines carry advertisements from distributors and vendors of professional education materials. If you can have your product reviewed by one or more trade journals, you'll benefit from the credibility of a respected and objective opinion and visibility that money can't buy. Of course this option carries with it the risk that the reviewer won't treat your project kindly, but the potential rewards are enormous. Another option is to enter your title in a professional competition. Be aware that there is often a time lag of several months between submission and presentation of awards, but an award-winning title can bring distributors knocking on your door, and pave the way for future titles.

Self help, how-to, and consumer education titles can be distributed through traditional book and video publishers. A good source for publishers is *The Writer's Marketplace*, a reference book for writers and publishers. You can also locate publishers by browsing at bookstores and libraries. These approaches will provide you with a list of publishers that carry works of similar genre and audience. Once you have identified several possibilities, make calls and write query letters to have your title reviewed for distribution.

Home entertainment is perhaps the most difficult market to enter. Wide visibility and distribution are needed, and the industry is very competitive. You can do research using consumer magazines and visit the video and consumer electronics stores to discover who is distributing what and which channels they are using. Some companies, such as Philips Interactive Media of America, distribute only CD-i and Video CD titles, and they are very aggressive in this technology. Others, such as Paramount Pictures, are involved in the technology as part of a widely diversified entertainment business.

Finally, self-distribution is an option. If your business is structured with marketing and sales professionals, you can order mass quantities of your title, advertise in your target market, and ship orders to customers directly.

The risks are large, the tension great, and the success is enormously gratifying. The careful market research that you conducted at the beginning of the project will provide you with such information as what your target audience reads, where they shop, and what they watch on TV. With this information, you can choose your advertising for the highest visibility among the consumers who will buy your titles.

TECHNICAL NOTES

TECHNICAL NOTES

The information in this chapter is the story behind MPEG digital video. When you understand how the compression is accomplished, you can move from a simple list of production do's and don'ts to an informed analysis of the video clips you'll encode. You'll know where problems are likely to show up in existing videos, and you can plan new videos to avoid the common encoding problems.

MPEG Explained

Digital video is, very simply, video frames translated by a computer into a series of ones and zeros. It's essentially no different from any other digital information. However, full-screen, full-motion digital video presents some new challenges. A single frame of video can occupy more than 5 or 6 million bytes of computer space. A single PhotoCD can only hold about 100 color photographs; without any audio, that translates to just over three seconds of motion video delivered at 30 frames per second. So the first problem with motion video becomes how to compress the information in the video frames to actually store a practical amount of video plus high-quality audio on a CD.

In August, 1993, the Motion Picture Experts Group approved a compression scheme that delivers 352 X 240 pixels of video at 29.97 frames per second. (For purposes of this discussion, we'll round that number up to 30 frames per second.) This compression scheme, called the MPEG1 code standard, describes not only the compression, but also the playback of compressed, or encoded, video. Compact discs can hold about 72 minutes of MPEG-compressed video and audio.

Bit Rates and Bandwidth
These two terms have basically the same meaning. Very simply, the allowable bandwidth is the budget allowed for data. Computers and CDs can move data at a very fast, but limited speed. Measured in bits per second or mega (millions of) bits per second, the bandwidth is the maximum amount of data that can move through a system. Single-speed compact disc drives can deliver data at a bandwidth of 1.15 million bits per second (1.15 MB/sec). 2X or higher CD drives can deliver data at higher rates. This difference is of no practical importance to digital video, since MPEG1 was designed for delivery from a single speed CD. A faster CD drive will not affect the display of an MPEG clip since the MPEG decoder controls the data delivery rates of the MPEG clip.

A large computer with a fast hard drive (usually an interactive TV server) can deliver data at a bandwidth of 5 million bits per second (5 MB/sec). If the bit rate for either MPEG1 or MPEG2 is exceeded, or the amount of data requires a higher bit rate, some data is lost. With audio data, this is typically heard as a mute or a skip. With video data, this is seen as dropped frames or visible artifacts. In severe cases, the video or audio may even stop playing and lock up or "crash" the player.

Digital Compression

Video tape delivers one full and complete picture to the monitor or TV screen every 30th of a second. When delivered at this speed, smooth, fluid motion is seen by the viewer. A full-screen frame of video can take up to 5 megabytes of data when digitized. Delivering that volume of data 30 times every second would require a data delivery mechanism that could move over 150 MB of data each second. Considering that a fast and capable hard disc drive today delivers about 5 MB per second and a CD can delivery data at 1.15 MB per second, full-screen, full-motion digital video was not achievable without fundamental changes in the delivery requirements of digital video. The delivery of information had to be re-designed so there was no perceptible loss of quality, no jerky silent-movie style motion, and no video noise.

The fundamental question became "How much information on each video frame is actually necessary?" By answering that question carefully and thoughtfully, the developers of the MPEG1 compression scheme could drastically reduce the storage space needed for continuous video footage. The solution to that question was answered in the form of three types of video frames: I-frames, P-frames, and B-frames. Within an average second of motion video, the 30 frames consist of 3 I-frames, 7 P-frames, and 20 B-frames. Together, these 30 frames represent a more than 200:1 compression over 30 standard frames of video. This level of compression allows playback of digital video at the required data delivery rates of 1.15 MB per second.

When a frame of video is encoded, it is divided into a grid of macro blocks. Each macro block is 8 pixels by 8 pixels square. When the encoder is compressing a frame of video and comparing the frame to previous and/or future frames, it is comparing a macro block at a time. So rather than an encoded frame containing information pixel by pixel, it contains information block by block. In pictures where there is a high degree of redundancy (a large expanse of sky for example), this technique also allows for even more compression by encoding a macro block at a time.

I-Frames (intra-frames) are full-screen, complete pictures. Each I-frame contains all the information needed to make a complete picture, and it is simply digitized block by block. I-frames are always the first frame displayed on the screen. This is true of the first frame at the start of a digital video sequence, as well as at the "jumping in" or entry points throughout the video. When using controls such as fast forward, reverse, and scan, the I-frames are the frames that are displayed and where video begins to play. Only I-frames contain enough information to display a complete picture.

P-Frames (predictive frames) consist of the differences from the I-frames. A P-frame contains only the information that has changed since the last I-frame, and describes pixel location, color luminescence, and brightness. When a scene is changing very rapidly, a P-frame may contain as much information an I-frame.

B-Frames (bi-directional frames) are similar in concept to animation morphing. B-frames are created when the computer looks back at the most recent I-frame, looks ahead to the differences described by a P-frame, then creates one or more B-frames between the I- and P-frames that describe the changes between the I- and P-frames. Despite the basic lack of honesty in a B-frame, they work amazingly well and contain even less information than the P-frames.

The difficulty in creating digital video comes in establishing how many of each type of frame is needed and possible. Obviously, using all I-frames would be ideal, but not possible. There's just too much information. Using just a few I-frames and a heavy dose of P- and B-frames allows great compression, but video quality suffers. Finding the optimal mix of frame types is the job of the digital video encoder system, and a good encoding system will allow some control over the placement of I-frames.

A typical encoding system creates I-, B-, and P- frames in the following sequence:

I B B P B B P B B P B B I ....

This sequence allows for an I-frame about every half second, and consequently, a complete scene change every half second. If the scene changes at a B- or P- frame, that B- or P- frame simply records the changes and carries an abnormally high amount of information. Typically, this creates no problem. Having an I-frame every half second also allows for a video "entry point" every half second. Entry points are points of time in a video sequence where a user can jump into the sequence. Fast forward, reverse, and interactive elements of a title depend on entry points to display a full and complete picture when the sequence is entered.

Encoding

When video is encoded, the order of pictures created is different from the order of pictures displayed during the decoding sequence when the video is played. To understand the difference between encoding and decoding, let's use a simple example of a linear video clip. The encoder reads in the first frame of video and encodes that complete picture. Then the encoder looks ahead to the frame that will be the next I-frame (the 15th frame) and encodes that complete picture. With two complete I-frames, the encoder then creates the P-frames that describe the differences between the first and second I-frames. With the P-frames encoded, the encoder then can look from frame to frame, backwards and forwards, to create the B-frames that fill in the gaps.

It's easy to understand how the encoder would have problems if the differences between two I-frames are massive. Since encoding relies on the redundancy between two frames to make accurate P- and B- frames, an extremely low amount of redundancy means very dense P- and B- frames and possible loss of information if the bandwidth is exceeded.

Audio Compression

Psycho acoustic models have shown that certain frequencies are not audible when other certain frequencies are present. This is called "masking." By sampling the audio at high rates (44.1 kHz/sec) and eliminating or reducing the masked frequencies in individual samples, the MPEG encoder can achieve an audio compression ratio of about 6:1 with no discernible loss in quality. The term most often used with MPEG-encoded audio is "CD-quality." Obviously, this is not the case, but the encoding algorithm is good enough that the difference between CD-quality and MPEG-encoded audio is discernible only by electronic analysis.

Simple Multiplexing
In this software process, the encoded audio and video files are "woven" (interleaved) into a single file. When audio and video files are multiplexed, the audio is inserted into the video stream at specific points identified by a timestamp. Multiplexing results in a single encoded audio/video bitstream.

Earlier during encoding, the video and audio are encoded separately, and each digital sample of encoded video and audio are given a timestamp. The timestamp identifies a relative position of the sample within a series of frames such as A1, A2, and A3 for the first three audio samples. The video frames are identified in the same way. The multiplexing software simply positions audio sample A1 with video sample V1, and so on to synchronize the audio and video.

Complex Multiplexing
Complex multiplexing is performed by the same software as simple multiplexing. Complex multiplexing allows for some interesting options. The MPEG specification allows up to 16 video and 32 audio files to be multiplexed into a single MPEG file. This allowance is useful for some specialized techniques, but is a dubious feature that should be used very carefully. It is also of no

use for Video CD, as the White Book specifies that video and audio must be encoded at specific bit rates. Those bit rates are high enough that there is only enough budget for a single video and single audio file in the video CD MPEG file. CD-i and CD-ROM have more liberal standards that allow you to multiplex several video and audio files into a single MPEG file.

When compressing video for MPEG, the better encoding systems allow you to specify the bit rate of the compressed file. The maximum encoded MPEG1 bandwidth is 1.5 MB/sec. If you are planning to multiplex two audio and two video clips in the same MPEG file, you must reduce the encoded bit rate of each by half. The video quality loss is significant at half the standard bit rate. To preserve picture quality, you can reduce the size of the picture by half, using only half of the screen.

Of more practical value is multiplexing one MPEG video file with more than one MPEG audio file. If the video bit rate is reduced by as little as 1 MB/sec, you would have room for 3 audio files that are encoded at 192 KB/sec. Using multiple audio files with a single video file allows you to develop multi-lingual applications or movies.

For MPEG2, multiplexing multiple audio and video files is a more practical technique. MPEG2 has a maximum bandwidth of 4.5 MB/sec. This bandwidth would allow three encoded MPEG1-quality video clips to be multiplexed into a single MPEG file. This technique is useful for interactive TV applications.

Common Problems

Animation Difficulties

On the surface, it seems that animations would be among the easiest materials to encode because of the limited range of color with large areas of redundancy. This has not proven to be the case, however, because of the high contrast in the material and the black outlines of the objects. When encoding existing animations, soften the contrast and scale down the black to make encoding easier. When developing animations for encoding, minimize the contrast and soften the edges of the objects. Avoid using saturated black outlines.

Colored Macro Blocking

This problem occurs when there is too much information in the encoded video stream. When the P-frames are very different from the closest I-frames, the amount of information in the video stream can exceed the capacity to deliver that information. When that happens, information gets lost and macro blocks in the frames show up as solid color blocks on the screen.

Shimmering

A jittery picture or shimmering is common in high contrast or fast moving scenes such as one showing running water. It is especially noticeable if the high contrast object takes a large amount of the screen. This is also caused by an excessive amount of changes from one frame to the next and if you take a close look at the jittery area, you'll see what looks like a degradation in the number of colors and some mosaic effect. A filter connected in line with the output of the VTR gives you the means to limit the dynamic range of the video by raising the black level and lowering the white level. Diminishing the chroma level sometimes helps as well as limiting the video bandwidth to between 3 and 4 MHz. Where sharp edges cause problems, you can soften the edges with an anti-aliasing filter.

I-frame Collisions

When creating a branch to a specific frame in a video clip, you must insert a custom I-frame at that point in the video. Since there is a regularly repeating I-frame interval (typically 12 or 15 frames apart), inserting "custom" I-frames can be a problem if a custom I-frame falls too close to a regularly repeating I-frame. This causes the video bit rate to exceed the buffer. To avoid this, an MPEG encoder that supports custom I-frame placement must not produce the regularly repeating I-frame, if the custom I-frame falls within 3 or fewer frames of what would normally be a regularly repeating I-frame.

Artifacts

Artifacts, also known as screen trash, are the result of video noise. The final MPEG stream's subjective quality in terms of visible artifacts is very source-content dependent and certain types of source material seem to generate more visible artifacts than others. In general, source material with a high degree of video noise produces more visible artifacts than softer, less noisy content such as film.

MPEG1 and MPEG2

MPEG1 and MPEG2 are fundamentally the same encoding/decoding standard. The difference lies in the bit rate at which they deliver data. MPEG1 was created specifically for delivery from a compact disc so it is encoded and decoded at the rate of 1.15 MB per second. MPEG2 was designed specifically for delivery from a server or hard disk drive and delivers data at the rate of 5 MB per second.

MPEG2 delivers the same number of frames per second but each picture can carry more than 4 times the amount of data. This translates to a higher quality picture — typically described as broadcast quality. MPEG2 encoded video is required for interactive TV applications.

The higher picture quality is a quantifiable measure. For subjective, practical purposes, MPEG1 video streams, if carefully produced and encoded, can deliver broadcast or near broadcast quality video. The feature movies produced by Paramount for CD-i are good examples of the high quality that is achievable by MPEG1.

Applications or presentations produced in the MPEG1 standard can be easily re-purposed for delivery in an MPEG2 environment. Since the only difference between the two standards is bit rate, an MPEG1 video stream can be converted with software to the MPEG2 standard.

TECHNIQUES

AND

EFFECTS

TECHNIQUES AND EFFECTS

Interactivity

Interactivity, involving branching to specific frames of a video sequence in MPEG applications, requires that the specific frame you wish to branch to is an I-frame with a sequence header attached (exactly like the first frame in an MPEG file). Since I-frames are repeated at regular intervals within an MPEG stream, simply including the sequence header information with each I-frame makes each I-frame look like the start of a stream to a given decoder.

If your interactive program requires that you branch to a specific frame in an MPEG stream, you will need to direct the MPEG compression system to insert a "custom" I-frame at the exact frame to which you need to branch. In this situation, I-frame collisions can be a problem. Be sure that your encoder can adjust for I-frames that are in close proximity.

Fast Branching

When data is delivered from a CD, the data in a file is not always continuous on a disc. When branching from the beginning of a movie to the middle, or from a Table of Contents screen to a specific scene, the delay caused by seeking for specific points in the file can sometimes be clumsy. A technique called fast branching can cut the delay times significantly.

Fast branching is best performed by supplying a separate index of the locations of entry points within the MPEG stream to the controlling program on the host platform. Entry points must be I-frames with a sequence header.

The index provides a map to a specific sector and byte where the beginning of the entry point resides. The controlling program can then instruct the CD drive or hard disk to jump directly to the specified track, sector, and byte, without searching for the frame or timecode. This method is particularly useful when delivering MPEG on a relatively slow medium such as a compact disc.

Authoring for this type of interactivity requires some method of identifying the specific frames and track/sector/byte placements of these entry points within the MPEG stream. Two methods are possible:

1. Instruct the MPEG encoder to output a byte offset index to specific entry points in the stream at encode time. This instruction is a simple option that you select with the encoder software. The byte offset index provides a map of the MPEG stream that contains the precise location of each entry point. With the byte offset index, the application software can access entry points directly by disc location rather than taking time to seek for the entry point.

2. Use a computer program to identify all I-frames in an MPEG stream, and create an index to the specific byte offsets to each entry point within the stream. This option works well on streams that have been previously encoded. It supplies the same information as the encoder generated byte offset index, but can be done later in the production process.

Full-featured mastering software will provide the options for either of these methods. The compact disc mastering tool must use the index created by one of these methods to produce the final track/sector/byte index file to be used by the controlling program.

Audio Techniques and Multilingual Audio

The MPEG audio specification (ISO 11172-3) provides for four different audio formats:
- Stereo,
- Joint stereo,
- Dual channel, and
- Mono.

Stereo is comprised of 2 channels, left and right. Stereo is suitable for phase encoded surround-sound applications, such as Dolby pro-logic.

Joint Stereo consists of 2 channels, left and right. Joint stereo uses redundancies of left and right channels to produce a subjectively higher quality at a given bit rate. This type of audio is most suitable for music applications. Phase-encoded surround sound will lose center channel information, but it provides excellent quality (comparable to 44.1 kHz PCM) for music at 192 kBps or higher.

117

Dual Channel contains 2 channels, 1 and 2. Dual channel audio discretely encodes channel 1 (left) and channel 2 (right). This audio type provides acceptable quality at 128 kBps, and excellent quality at higher bit rates (224 kBps or higher). It is most suitable for multilingual and Karaoke applications.

Mono includes only 1 channel, discretely encoded. This audio type provides excellent quality at low bit rates and is well-suited for narration.

Note: According to the White Book specification, if dual channel encoding is employed on a White Book Video CD, Video CD players will output either channel 1 or channel 2 in mono through both left and right outputs and will offer a means of selecting which channel to monitor. If the stream is STEREO or JOINT STEREO, then the Video CD player will play the audio in full stereo. Mono is not supported in Video CD.

Seamless Branching

Seamless branching is a very exciting feature that allows seamless switching between MPEG clips (without delay, and imperceptibly) within an interactive application. Seamless branching is a difficult and complex feature to implement, but can be spectacular for certain applications, especially consumer games and demanding training applications. An excellent game example is the CD-i version of *Mad Dog McCree* by CapDisc.

Seamless branching can be achieved by multiplexing two or more video and audio streams into a single multiplexed MPEG file. While playing the multiplexed MPEG stream through a decoder, the controlling program can simply select which video or audio stream to play, based on user input.

On the surface, this seems simple enough, but consider the I-, B-, P- picture structure and the buffer status of the decoder hardware at branch time.

Since the decoding of MPEG P- and B- pictures depends on past or future pictures for decompression, arbitrarily jumping to another bitstream is likely to cause visible, if not fatal, decoder errors.

To successfully achieve a seamless branch, the two video and audio bitstreams must have identical picture types and buffer status at the branch point. The branch must occur when both bitstreams contain an I-frame.

To complicate the issue, consideration must also be given to the bandwidth of the delivery medium. Since two or more video and audio streams must be delivered to the decoder hardware simultaneously, this effectively doubles the bandwidth requirements to play back the multiplexed stream. In the case of a single-speed CD (such as CD-i), it would appear that seamless branching would be bandwidth-prohibitive for a single-speed CD medium.

Fortunately, there is a way. On a low-bandwidth medium such as CD-i, seamless branching can be achieved in two ways:

Method 1. Reduce the audio and video bit rates for each stream; the sum of them cannot exceed the maximum available bandwidth of the medium. This method works, but at a significant sacrifice of quality.

Method 2. Reduce the number of encoded pixels in each stream, proportional to the percentage of maximum bandwidth available to each stream. In other words, if:

Maximum bandwidth = 1.4 Mb/second
Bit rate required for acceptable video quality = 1.4 Mb/second (at full 352 x 240 pixel screen size)
Number of multiplexed streams = 2

Reduce screen size to 352 x 120 (1/2 the number pixels). Encode both streams at .7 Mb/second each. Multiplex both streams for a total of 1.4 Mb/second.

Obviously, the example above leaves 50% of the pixels of the video field blank. Usually, an interactive game or other program will have other graphics on the screen while playing MPEG video. In the case cited above, the bottom half of the screen could be a graphic overlay of a control panel or automobile dashboard, concealing this deficiency. Several CD-i titles employ seamless branching in this manner.

There is another method to achieve a seamless branch that is simple and effective. This method is not technically a seamless branch, but it effectively masks the time it takes to load a new video clip. It also demands that branches are made at discreet times, rather than any time the viewer chooses.

1. Play the video clip.
2. Load a still image that is a copy of the last frame of video.
3. Display viewers' choices.
4. Load and play chosen video clip that is a continuation of the previous video.

For example, a title that shows a tour on city streets could stop at a traffic light and switch to a still image that displays left and right arrows for choice of direction to turn. After the viewer makes the choice, the next video clip begins at the same traffic light but turns in the direction that the viewer chose. This method can be used in many different types of titles as long as you produce carefully to mask the seek delay when switching to a new clip. The seek delay from the end of one clip to the beginning of another takes about 2 seconds.

Other seamless branching techniques are possible, including pre-loading the decoder buffer, but will require the expertise of a programmer to manipulate the data at very low levels.

Forward and Reverse Scanning

Forward and reverse scanning is generally performed by seeking to and decoding only I-frames in an MPEG stream. I-frame intervals in MPEG1 streams are typically located at 1/3 to 1/2 second intervals.

The seek intervals vary with the controlling application. The White Book (Video CD) specification states that 2 seconds is adequate for forward and reverse scan intervals. Other mediums may scan at different intervals.

Using a fast-seek delivery medium (such as a hard disk), forward and reverse scan in MPEG is not much of a problem, due to the fact that a hard disk can seek to another track/sector faster than the decoder buffer runs out of audio/video data.

A compact disc, however, cannot seek faster than the speed of the MPEG data so another method has to be employed for forward and reverse scanning. The method involves the use of an I-frame index file which contains a track, sector, and byte offset index to every entry point (I-frame with sequence header) in the MPEG stream.

This index provides an accurate map of the disc so the controlling application can jump directly to a specific track and sector where the next entry point resides, eliminating the need to search for the next entry point.

Creating this index is generally the responsibility of the pre-mastering software. In the case of CD-i, the most popular pre-mastering engines will automatically create an I-frame index when copying the MPEG streams to the disc.

Types
of
Encoding
Systems

TYPES OF ENCODING SYSTEMS

There are basically four types of encoding systems available in four distinct price ranges.

The High End

At the very top of the market is IBM's Power Visualization System. This is a million-dollar encoding system that processes the highest quality possible MPEG video. It is without argument the highest quality system in the world, as well as the most expensive. It is not a real-time encoding system. One minute of video requires two hours to encode, but the encoded video is as close to broadcast quality as is possible with MPEG.

Mid-Range Systems

The two systems that occupy the middle of the price range (\$25,000 – \$75,000) are both real-time desktop encoding systems. You can choose between either a component or composite video system. The only significant difference between these two available encoding systems is the MPEG compression engine. The better quality (and more expensive) systems use a professional, broadcast-quality 4:4:4 component video capture and display system. The less expensive systems use S-video or composite video capture and display.

A component desktop system will cost in the neighborhood of $75,000, and the composite video systems cost between $25,000 and $40,000. The variance in price is more due to features and support than actual system quality.

Since the quality of the MPEG-encoded video is directly related to the quality of the source, the component-based encoding systems will produce consistently higher-quality digital video than the composite-based systems. Since composite video produces more noise than component video, the composite systems may also require more post production editing of the tape and filtering at the encoder input to avoid screen artifacts or macro-blocking.

These disadvantages do not necessarily make the composite systems a poor choice. The major advantage to the composite systems is that they cost at least 50% less than the component systems, and the subjective quality of the encoded streams is quite good.

Low Budget Options

At the low end of the encoding system spectrum is the XingIt! board from Xing Technology that produces quarter-screen MPEG video. Also available as shareware are the software-only encoders that provide little or no control of encoding process and quality. The low-end encoding systems can be purchased for less than $1,000.

Making Your Selection

In the current market, the four types of encoding systems appeal to four distinct target markets. The million-dollar systems are used by motion picture production companies and a few digital video service bureaus. The component systems are owned by film and video producers as well as service bureaus that provide encoding services by contract. The composite systems are ideal for industrial use in companies that produce training videos for internal use and educational videos for commercial distribution. A low-end system may be a good option for developers who need higher quality than QuickTime or Video for Windows, but do not need full-screen video.

WORDS
OF
WISDOM
FROM
MPEG
EXPERTS

WORDS OF WISDOM
FROM MPEG EXPERTS

Mr. Bob Auger,
Managing Director at Electric Switch Limited

"the first important message is *make the source video to as high a standard as you can, within your budget* . . . Analog Component video formats, like Betacam SP, are ideal as a source for an MPEG encoder . . .VHS or Hi8 cannot be considered as the best input format for MPEG video."

"MPEG will look its best when the whole production process has been in the digital domain, as long as it is *component* digital . . . D1, D5, Digital Betacam, and so on, are perfect source machines for an MPEG encoder, particularly when coupled with a noise reduction system such as the BTS MNR10."

"Film is the ideal source for an MPEG encoder, as long as you make a graded transfer to a component digital VTR from a telecine with the minimum film weave.

"Black and White film, even archive material, can look excellent, with no color bias or artifacts and perfect grey scale reproduction. Color film, particularly using low-grain stock, is possibly the best way of acquiring images for MPEG encoding and, for those with the necessary skills, it represents the ideal input format.

"In other words, post produce film as normal, transfer it to tape in the finest telecine suite you can afford (go on, use a wet-gate steady-film telecine!) and take that to your preferred encoding house. The result will be the best that MPEG can offer."

Mr. David Cunningham
Digital Media Studios

When producing video for MPEG conversion:

"Stay fully component where ever possible (Beta SP or D1)"

"Avoid: High contrast, high chroma, lots of motion, fades, dissolves, short edges as in computer animations, noise, small, anti-aliased type, explosions, backlit water, busy patterns, sharp diagonal lines."

"When shooting film, edit in film, not transferred video. Do not edit the video after telecine."

Mr. Dieter Schleutmann
Telemedia

For the best results when producing video for MPEG encoding:

"No composite video!"

"Use material as close to the source as possible."

"No content with many details, moving leaves in the woods, etc."

"No soft fades, fast movements, or standards converted materials (PAL converted to NTSC, or NTSC converted to PAL)."

"Ideal: Digital scanning of 35 mm film to D1 tapes."

THE
COLOR
BOOKS

THE COLOR BOOKS

Compact discs are governed by a set of specifications known informally as the "color books". These books specify the technical details of the various CD formats such as disc layout, lead-in, lead-out, allowable file types, error detection, control data, etc. The adoption of a formal specification for the different CD types has been the major reason that CDs can remain a low cost and reliable format for data storage and retrieval.

There are five specifications (Color Books) that govern the major compact disc formats:

Red Book	Audio CDs
Yellow Book	CD-ROM
Green Book	CD-i
Orange Book	Recordable CDs (Write Once and MagnetoOptical)
White Book	Video CD

Other CD formats exist, and are specified by derivative specifications based on one or more of the above standards. Some of the other formats include:

Mixed Mode	Different data standards on the same disc, for example, audio and computer data

CD-ROM XA CD-ROM extended architecture.

CD-i Bridge Compatible with CD-i and CD-ROM XA such as Photo CD.

Hybrid Combination ISO 9660 and Macintosh HFS file formats

3DO Special format for 3DO game machines.

The types of CDs that can contain MPEG compressed digital video include CD-ROM, Mixed Mode, CD-ROM XA, Hybrid, CD-i, CD-i Bridge, Video CD, and 3DO.

Compact Disc Architecture
A compact disc was first described by the Red Book specification in 1980. The Red Book is the basic CD specification on which all other specification are derived. The basic architecture of the CD that was specified in the Red Book does not differ from the newer CD formats. A CD consists of three basic divisions:

Lead In Area Contains data describing the contents of the disc (Table of Contents (TOC) file) and where each track starts.

Program Area Contains up to 99 tracks of information, allowing for about 6750 MB of user data storage.

Lead Out Area   Buffer in case the player reads past the last track.

Each of the 99 tracks in the program area are subdivided into sectors that are 1/75th of a second in length, and holds 2,353 bytes of digital data. In an audio CD, all 2,353 bytes of data are digital audio data. The Red Book defined a single type of track for audio CDs. That track is CD-Digital Audio (CD-DA).

CD-ROM

The CD-ROM format was defined by the Yellow Book in 1984. A CD-ROM is a compact disc that contains digital computer data. There are two primary types of CD-ROM discs: ISO 9660 and Macintosh HFS. ISO 9660 is a universal file format designed for CD-ROM that can be read by a variety of computers, such as DOS, Windows, UNIX, and Apple computers. An ISO 9660 disc can contain files and executable programs for several different computers on the same disc. For example, an ISO 9660 disc may contain executable programs for a PC, a Macintosh, and a UNIX workstation and a single collection of data files that can be accessed by each executable program. This way, the same CD-ROM disc can run on a variety of different computer types and access the same data. The important thing to remember when creating an ISO 9660 disc for cross platform use, is that the data files must be in a format that all computers can recognize.

A Macintosh HFS disc contains the same file structure as Macintosh computers, and when viewed on a Macintosh, the CD-ROM is graphically represented just like a hard disk drive or floppy disk drive. The advantage to using the HFS structure over the ISO 9660 structure is that the HFS structure maintains the familiar "Mac" look and feel" to the desktop for CD-ROMs that will be marketed only for Macintosh users. The HFS structure is also less restrictive with file naming conventions.

The Yellow Book standard extends the Red book by defining two more types of tracks in addition to the CD-DA tracks: Mode 1, and Mode 2. Like audio CDs, these tracks are subdivided into 2,352-byte sectors. The Yellow Book also adds some restrictions to the sectors. Mode 1 tracks, the most common type of CD-ROM data contain 12 bytes of synchronization data, 4 bytes of header information, 2,048 bytes of user data, 4 bytes of error detection, 8 bytes blank, and 276 bytes error correction. The sync and header bytes allow the computer to identify which sector is being read. The last 288 bytes following the user data provide the increased error detection and correction needed for computer data.

Mode 2 tracks are usually used for compressed audio, video, and picture data and are typically used for CD-ROM XA. Mode 2 tracks do not require the 288 bytes of error detection and correction in each sector. This allows 2,336 bytes of user data to be stored in each sector. Mode 2 CD-ROM tracks that are not CD-ROM

XA are extremely rare and require special decoding software to be readable.

MPEG data are typically stored in Mode 1 CD-ROM tracks. MPEG data is stored in tracks that are separate from the executable program and any other type of digital data and are preceded by a "pre-gap" of 2 seconds (150 sectors). The pre-gap is consists of all zeros and helps transition between tracks of differing data types. The pre-gap is not required between MPEG tracks, since they are the same data type. The pre-gap is automatically built into the disc by the disc recording software, but will affect the total available storage area on the disc. When developing applications for CD-ROM, be sure to account for the 2 second pre-gap pause between two differing file types. This will affect the timing and play of your title.

Mixed Mode
A mixed mode disc is a CD-ROM disc with digital audio (CD-DA) tracks added. The most common type of mixed mode disc has computer data in the first track, followed by digital audio tracks on the remainder of the disc. The data track usually contains a control program that accesses the audio tracks. Since only one track can be accessed by the CD-ROM drive at a time, the program must either be read and stored in the computer's active memory (RAM) while the audio tracks play, or the audio must stop playing during program access and execution.

When MPEG files are located on the same disc with audio tracks, the MPEG files are stored in separate and distinct tracks. The CD-DA tracks cannot be played while the MPEG tracks are playing, and the MPEG tracks cannot be accessed while the CD-DA tracks play.

CD-ROM XA

CD-ROM XA is an extension to the Yellow Book that allows video, audio, and data to be accessed at the same time. While a standard CD-ROM must have video, audio, and data files located in separate tracks, the CD-ROM XA standard provides for "interleaving" these data types. The audio files used on a CD-ROM XA disc are Adaptive Pulse Code Modulated (ADPCM) audio files, not CD-DA files. ADPCM audio files are compressed audio files and can be either stereo or mono files.

Interleaving is similar to multiplexing. Compact discs can deliver data at a rate of 1.14 MB per second. Level A stereo ADPCM audio, for example, must be delivered at 85 kB per second. That leaves just over 1 MB per second of data remaining that can be delivered. By interleaving the audio with a video image, the audio can begin playing at the same time the video is delivered to the computer screen. As the audio continues, text can be overlaid on the video image.

CD-ROM XA discs subdivide the 2,352 byte sector somewhat differently than CD-ROMs. CD-ROM XA requires an 8-byte subheader preceding the 2048 bytes of user data. The 8 bytes of blank data is eliminated in the XA format so there is no loss of available user data. The subheader contains information a file ID number to identify all the sectors belonging to the same file, a channel number that identifies what type of data is interleaved, submode attributes (for selection and allocation control), and coding information that identifies the type of data in the user area.

Most CD-ROM drives must have additional hardware to play XA discs. Since the XA format contains specific types of compressed digital data, the XA hardware contains the proper decoding and decompression circuits for output to the speakers and computer.

The MPEG format is fully compatible with XA players, provided the players are equipped with MPEG decoder circuits.

Hybrid

A Hybrid disc contains more than one file system. The most common type of hybrid disc contains an ISO 9660 component and a Macintosh HFS component. These discs can be played on both PCs and Macs, and each computer will recognize it's native file system and ignore the other.

A hybrid disc can be effectively divided in half, with each half of the disc containing a separate file system. Using this method, you have effectively half of the disc storage space devoted to each file system. Another method of creating hybrid discs is to share data between the two file systems. In this method, you can have executable programs that are native to each file system, but use the same data files for both file systems. This is done by using aliases. To use aliases, you first create the Macintosh file structure with the Macintosh program and data files. Then, using the "Make Alias" feature in the multifinder "File" menu, you create aliases for the data files and drag the aliases into the ISO 9660 folder where the PC application resides. Then, when the PC application runs, it calls the data files that reside in the Macintosh file system. As long as the data files are of a format compatible to both PC and Macintosh computers, the process is simple and allows much more efficient use of disc space.

CD-i

CD-i, Compact Disc-interactive, was a CD format and standard released in 1987. It is governed by the Green Book specification. CD-i is a fully interactive multimedia platform that consists of a stand-alone player connected to a TV set. CD-i avoids the limitations of CD-ROM by taking advantage of file interleaving. The Green book specifies how data and compressed audio are interleaved in the same track, which allows high quality audio to play at the same time data is being accessed. The result is a compact disc format that allows full interactivity and real-time access to video and audio data.

The layout of a CD-i disc is identical to CD-ROM XA with an 8-byte subheader and 2048 bytes of user data in each sector. CD-i discs can also be mixed mode discs, including "Red" non-compressed digital audio tracks in tracks separate from the CD-i application. The CD-i tracks are not included in the TOC file in the lead in area, so when a CD-i disc is played in an audio CD player, the data tracks are not played, which could damage stereo speakers.

CD-i was the first CD format to adopt the MPEG format for full motion video files. The authoring software for CD-i development includes the capability to play and control MPEG files. CD-i players must be equipped with digital video circuitry or an add-on cartridge to play titles containing MPEG digital video.

CD-i Bridge

The CD-i Bridge disc is a CD-ROM XA disc that contains extensions that allow the XA disc to be played on both CD-i players and CD-ROM XA drives such as Photo CD players, 3DO players, Karaoke players, and CD-ROM XA drives connected to a computer. A Kodak Photo CD disc is an example of a CD-i Bridge disc.

This cross compatibility of CD-ROM XA is not comprehensive. For example, you can play a photo CD on a Photo CD player or a 3DO player, but you cannot play a 3DO disc on a Photo CD player.

A CD-i Bridge disc must conform to both the Green Book and the XA extension to the Yellow Book. Both CD-i discs and CD-ROM XA discs contain a volume descriptor that is located at a specific point on the finished disc. The volume descriptor defines where the directory structure on the disc starts. A Bridge disc must contain both a CD-i volume descriptor and a CD-ROM XA volume descriptor. Since the volume descriptors for each type of disc is located at a different specific point on the disc, they both may be present without overlap. When the disc is played on a CD-i player, the XA volume descriptor is ignored. When played on an XA player, the CD-i volume descriptor is ignored.

Like CD-i discs, the CD-i track is not included in the Table of Contents file. When played on an audio CD player, the CD-i track will not be recognized as existing, so audio equipment is protected from possible damage from playing a data track. The XA track is listed in the TOC file so that it can be played by XA-compatible players. The disc layout of a CD-i Bridge disc is identical to CD-i and CD-ROM XA discs.

Video CD

Video CD is defined by the White Book specification. The White Book specification was developed from the original Karaoke CD specification to provide for a wider range of full-motion video applications than simply Karaoke. The White Book specification was developed by Philips and JVC, and is supported by Sony and

Matsushita as well. Video CDs are primarily feature-length digital video and does not involve a high level of interactivity.

Video CDs are a form of CD-i Bridge discs, so they can be played on CD-i, CD-ROM XA, and Video CD players. The disc layout is identical to CD-i and CD-ROM XA.

Video CDs take advantage of MPEG1 digital video. The discs contain a CD-i application that provides the movie controls such as Play, Stop, Pause, Fast Forward, Reverse, Slow Scan forward and reverse. These controls are displayed on the screen when the view presses a button on the remote. Pressing the button again hides the control panel. When played on a Video CD player, the on-screen control panel is not needed. All controls are provided on the hand-held remote control and on the front panel of the player.

Another feature of Video CDs is the menus or table of contents screens. Video CDs can contain still images and index points. Used together, developers can create still image screens that list major scenes in a movie like chapters in a book. By selecting a scene from a menu, viewers can take advantage of the random-access nature of CDs and jump immediately to different locations in the movie without having to fast forward and reverse through the scenes, or keep track of tape index numbers. Video CD was the first format developed exclusively for MPEG digital video. The typical Video CD consists of an MPEG video file, a CD-i control application, and still images containing the chapter lists or table of contents. The authoring software for Video CD allows the developer to specify a list of chapters that is used by the table of contents screen to jump to sections of the video.

3DO

The 3DO Interactive Multiplayer is primarily a games machine that delivers high quality graphics and real-time interactivity. A 3DO disc is a type of CD-ROM XA disc and conforms to the XA extension of the Yellow Book. 3DO discs are compatible only with the dedicated 3DO player. The player, however, recognizes and will play other CD-ROM XA discs such as CD-DA, Photo CD, and CD+Graphics. When equipped with a digital video cartridge, the player also plays 3DO applications that use MPEG digital video and Video CDs.

The 3DO player contains a double-speed CD-ROM XA drive. When playing MPEG files, the transfer of MPEG data is controlled by the decoder circuits in the digital video cartridge rather than by the speed of the drive. MPEG files will play correctly regardless of whether the drive is single speed, double speed, or faster. This guarantees compatibility across a wide range of hardware types.

Disc Mastering

CD-i, CD-i Bridge, CD-ROM XA, and Video CD all make use of interleaved audio, video, and data files. Interleaving enables different file types to exist within the same track and allows these different file types to be played simultaneously. Each of these disc types also require that specific information be located in the lead-in area of the disc.

Disc mastering software is required when making a CD-i, CD-i Bridge, CD-ROM XA, and Video CD. An authored application consists of either a text file or computer program that identifies all the separate images, animation, audio, MPEG and menu files and instructions for when to play, how long to play, which transition effects to use, and how to respond to user input. The mastering software reads these instructions then creates the lead-in information and builds the interleaved files. The files are then compiled into a single file that will be croded in a single track on a CD.

CD-ROM applications do not require disc mastering before recording. The authored title contains the instructions for program operation, and the image, animation, audio, and MPEG files remain in separate and distinct files. These files often reside in different tracks on the CD. When a CD ROM application is played, the application instructions determine which files are needed at specific times, then seeks and opens the correct files. If, for example, an audio file and an animation file must play simultaneously, there must be sufficient computer memory (RAM) to store and play the audio while the animation is splayed from the CD.

MPEG files are the exception. Because MPEG files are multiplexed audio and video, both reside in the same file and can play at the same time, perfectly synchronized. You can take advantage of this ability when computer memory is critical by encoding slide shows with audio or animation with audio and making MPEG files for precisely synchronized playback. By simply transferring the video and audio sequences to video tape, you create the source material for the MPEG encoder.

Interleaving and Multiplexing

Two methods of combining video and audio in the same file have been described: interleaving and multiplexing. These two methods are quite similar; both involve taking advantage of the full bandwidth available to combine two or more separate files in the same digital stream. There is a critical difference between interleaving and multiplexing that is important to understand.

Interleaving is the process of combining separate audio, image, animation, and/or movies into a single file that optimizes the full bandwidth of the CD. Multiplexing reads the timecodes built into the audio and video files and synchronizes the timecodes while combining the files into the same data stream. Interleaving does not synchronize the files. When there is a need to precisely synchronize audio and video in interleaved files, as in "talking heads"-style clips, the synchronization must be managed by the authoring tool.

More Information

Red Book Yellow Book ISO9660	American National Standards Institute 1430 Broadway New York, NY 10018 Sales Department: (212) 642-4900
Green Book	CD-i Association of North America 11111 Santa Monica, Suite 700 Los Angeles, CA 90025 (310) 444-6613
White Book Orange Book	Mr. Burt Gall PCE Coordination Office P.O. Box 80002 5600 JB Eindhoven, The Netherlands

INTERACTIVE TV

INTERACTIVE TV

Interactive TV is truly an infant industry. One of the popular buzz words describing the technology is "convergence", referring to the convergence of television, computers, and telephone into a single friendly, interactive medium for homes. Interactive TV relies on MPEG technology to fulfill its promises. MPEG digital video technology offers the means to deliver multiple video and audio files quickly and cleanly to the TV set-top decoder boxes.

Trials are being conducted by cable, telephone, and computer companies that test everything from ITV channel delivery methods, server types, and set-top decoders, to types of interactive programming that the public wants. The question of "What is Interactive TV" is still largely undefined and unanswerable. The programming possibilities are enormous – from the simplest implementation of video on demand, to interactive game shows played by millions of people across the country, to personal banking and financial management. The question of "What is possible?" is less an issue than a more pragmatic "What will sell, and where do we start?" Although those larger questions will be answered only in time, there are some more basic issues that can be introduced here to give you a fundamental understanding about how interactive TV works.

An Interactive TV network consists of a computer server located at a central station, and set-top decoders (set-top box) located in the subscriber's home. The server and set-top box are connected via telephone cable or (in time) a fiber-optic or cable network.

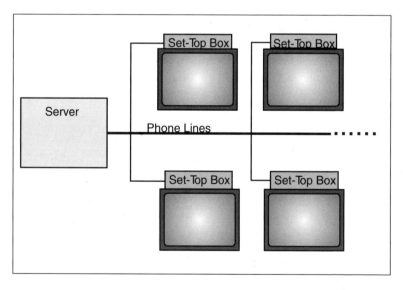

Interactive TV Server–Viewer Diagram

The interactive TV server is a large, powerful computer

that stores program applications and data files. The program applications are very similar to interactive multimedia applications. The set-top box looks similar to a VCR and connects to the TV through a simple cable. A remote control much like a standard TV remote control lets the users select items from menus and otherwise communicate with the program. The server and set-top boxes are connected by common T1 phone lines that provide the two-way communication between users and the program applications.

In a more complex system, the set-top boxes have built-in features or can connect to magnetic card readers (like a credit card reader), printers, and other peripheral devices that extend the programming options to allow in-home ATM transactions, print invoices, charge merchandise and issue credit card receipts, and print transcripts or research material from on-line libraries.

An Interactive TV development system consists of a desk-top computer connected to server/set-top system. The desk-top computer runs the authoring and development software. When applications are developed, they are transferred to the server for testing. The server/set-top system used for development is identical to the commercially used system described above, except smaller in scale, so testing can be done on a system that accurately reflects the actual delivery environment.

Application development for interactive TV is very

much the same as multimedia development. Digital video, still image, animations, audio, and text are developed just as they are for interactive multimedia, converted to the specific formats used for interactive TV, then authored into an application using some of the same authoring tools. Of all interactive multimedia formats, CD-i is the closest to interactive TV. The still image and audio formats used are identical, and CD-i authoring tools are highly compatible with interactive TV.

The biggest difference between development for CD-i or other multimedia formats and development for interactive TV is in the disc building stage. Rather than compile a disc image for recording, the final developed application is compiled in a format that has been optimized for delivery from the server.

Interactive TV uses a form of MPEG digital video called MPEG2. MPEG2 is fundamentally identical to MPEG1, except that MPEG2 data is "packaged" for delivery at data rates of 4.5 MB/second rather than the MPEG1 rates of 1.14 MB/second, and involves some optimization for delivery from a server rather than a CD. Converting existing MPEG1 files to MPEG2 files is a relatively simple process controlled by software, or another option is to have the source video re-encoded using MPEG2 standards. The production and editing are the same for MPEG1 and MPEG2.

The encoding systems for MPEG1 and MPEG2 are

nearly identical. The primary difference lies in the encoder and decoder cards; MPEG2 requires a different and larger set of encoder and decoder chips than an MPEG1 encoder.

Interactive multimedia applications that have been developed for delivery from a CD can be re-purposed for delivery from an interactive TV server. This process is easiest for CD-i and Video CD applications, since the file formats and authoring systems are virtually identical. CD-ROM applications must be converted to the audio and image formats used for interactive TV, then authored and compiled using an interactive TV authoring system such as OptImage's MediaMogul or a programming language with the required interactive TV extensions. Custom programming interactive TV applications can currently be written using the operating system extensions developed and sold by Microware Systems Corporation. Popular CD-ROM authoring software like Macromedia's Director, are good prototyping tools for Interactive TV, but don't yet provide a complete path to Interactive TV application development.

As the technology develops and the trials continue, the market will become defined in terms of services that are needed by consumers. Consequently, the server, set-top boxes, and development systems will expand to include the features that take advantage of the converging technologies of computers, telephone, and television.

Resources

RESOURCES

EDUCATION AND TRAINING

Georgia Institute of Technology, Department of Continuing Education, Center for NewMedia Education and Research
Multimedia Series and Certificate in Multimedia
P.O. Box 93636
Atlanta, Georgia 30377
Phone: (404) 894-2400
Fax: (404) 894-8925

Microware Systems Corporation
DAVID (Digital Audio/Video Interactive Decoder) is a system architecture for interactive TV networking and set-top devices.
DAVID Training for Set-TOP/Server Manufacturers
DAVID Training for Authoring Tools/Application Developers
1900 N.W. 114th St.
Des Moines, Iowa 50325-7077
Phone: (515) 224-1929
Fax: (515) 224-1352

OptImage Interactive Services
Introduction to Interactive TV Authoring
Authoring with Digital Video
Digital Video Encoding
Introduction to CD-i and MediaMogul
Multimedia: A Designer's Perspective
  7185 Vista Drive
  West Des Moines, Iowa 50266-9313
  Phone: (800) 234-5484
  Fax: (515) 225-0252

Philips Interactive Media Centre
Digital Video Principles
Digital Video Hands-on Delta Vx
CD-i Design Principles
CD-i Programming with MediaMogul
CD-i Programming with Balboa
  Maastrichterstraat 63
  3500 Hasselt - Belgium
  Phone: +32 11 242 546
  Fax: +32 11 242 168

DIGITAL VIDEO SYSTEMS AND SOFTWARE COMPANIES

3DO
Desktop digital video encoding system
  600 Galveston Dr.
  Roseville, CA 94063
  Phone: (415) 261-3211
  Fax: (415) 261-3230

CeQuadrat

Desktop digital video encoding system
5 Thomas Mellon Circle, Suite 105
San Francisco, CA 94134
Phone: (415) 715-5610
Fax: (415) 715-5619

High Technology Smart & Friendly

Software-only encoding system
16539 Saticoy St.
Van Nuys CA 91406
Phone: (818) 994-8001
Fax: 988-6581

IPC Technologies

Desktop digital video encoding system
10300 Metric Blvd
Austin, TX 78758
Phone: (512) 339-3500
Fax: (512) 454-1357

Microware Systems Corporation

Interactive TV system architecture
Set-top decoders
1900 N.W. 114th St.
Des Moines, Iowa 50325-7077
Phone: (515) 224-1929
Fax: (515) 224-1352

Optibase
Video CD authoring systems
5000 Quorum Drive, Suite 700
Dallas, TX 75240
Phone: (214) 239-5242
Fax: (214) 239-1273

OptImage Interactive Services
Interactive TV/CD-i application authoring system
Video CD authoring system
Desktop digital video encoding systems
7185 Vista Drive
West Des Moines, Iowa 50266
Phone: (800) 234-5484
Fax: (515) 225-0252

Optivision
Desktop digital video encoding system
4009 Miranda Ave
Palo Alto, CA 94304
Phone: (415) 855-0200
Fax: (415) 855-0222

Philips Interactive Media Systems NV
Interactive TV/CD-i application authoring system
Video CD authoring system
Desktop digital video encoding systems
Maastrichterstraat 63
3500 Hasselt - Belgium
Phone: +32 11 242 546
Fax: +32 11 242 168

DIGITAL VIDEO SERVICES

Backs Electronic Publishing Ltd.
MPEG digital encoding
CD-ROM software development
CD-i software development
Video CD software development
Creative graphics animations
Programmer's tooklit (for CD-i and CD-ROM)
    Old Manse Guestwick
    Norfolk, NR20 5QJ, UK
    Phone +44 1362 684444
    Fax: +44 1362 638835

Interactive Resources
MPEG encoding
On-site production for digital video segments
Consulting and custom programming
    2708 Grand Ave., Suite C
    Des Moines, IA 50312
    Phone: (515) 288-9259
    Fax: (515) 288-9263

SITC (Scottish Interactive Technology Centre)
MPEG encoding in PAL and NTSC
CD-i authoring
Interactive TV authoring
Specializing in educational titles
    Moray House Institute
    Holyroad Road
    Edinburgh, EH8 8AQ UK
    Phone: +44 1 31 558 6700
    Fax: +44 1 31 557 2005

Stokes Interactive
Pre-production source tape conversion/editing
Pre-production sequence definition
MPEG encoding
Video CD design and authoring
CD recording
5642 Dyer St.
Dallas, TX 75206
Phone: (214) 363-0161
Fax: (214) 363-8871

U.S. Digital Video/dhg Productions, Inc./SR Audio
Video and film production
Post-production editing
Custom graphics
Video targeting and positioning
Audio production and editing
Sound FX/production music
Custom music scoring
2771 104th St.
Urbandale, IA 50322
Phone: (515) 276-9693
Fax: (515) 276-1825

Philips Interactive Media Centre
Title testing for specification compliance – CD-i
and Video CD
Maastrichterstraat 63
3500 Hasselt - Belgium
Phone: +32 11 242 546
Fax: +32 11 242 168

Lost Boys Interactive
Title production for CD-i, CD-ROM, Video CD
Keizersgrach 16g
1016 Dp Amsterdam, Holland
Phone: +31 20 420 3371
Fax: +31 20 420 3356

Electric Switch Limited
MPEG 1 encoding
MPEG 1 and 2 multiplexing
Cinepak/Indeo encoding
Fractal video encoding
3D graphics production
VR production
Motion capture
Motion control
Prototyping
Consulting
7-11 Lexington St.
London, W1R 3HQ
Phone: +44 (0) 171 437 4402
Fax: +44 (0) 171 437 4403

Telemedia/Bertelsmann
Video tape editing
Preprocessing/denoising of video and audio
MPEG encoding
Authoring on several platforms and levels
Graphic design
Animations
Title design
Audio editing and recording
Carl Bertelsmann St. 161
33311 Güetersloh, Germany
Phone: +49 5241 80 5017
Fax: +49 5241 80 6071

Disc Manufacturing, Inc.
Compact disc replication for all formats
CD-ROM and CD-i disc formatting
Mastering
    1409 Foulk Road, Suite 102
    Wilmington, DE 19803
    Phone: 1 (800) 433-DISC
    Fax: (302) 479-2527

Encoding Services:
Backs Electronic Publishing Ltd.
MPEG digital encoding
CD-ROM software development
Video CD development
CD-i software development
Video CD software development
Creative graphics animations
Programmers toolkit for CD-i and CD-ROM title
development
    The Old Manse Guestwick
    Norfolk, NR20 5QJ, UK
    Phone: +44 1362 684444
    Fax: +44 1362 683835

Digital Media Studios
MPEG1 and MPEG2 Encoding
Custom Video Pre-processing
Specializing in high quantity encoding
    660 White Plains Road
    Tarrytown, New York 10591
    Phone: (914) 524-5200
    Fax: (914) 524-5233

AVM Aktiengesellschaft
MPEG Encoding
Video CD Production
CD-i development
CD-ROM development
Kägenstrasse 17
CH-4153 Reinach, Switzerland
Phone: +41 61 716 90 70
Fax: +41 61 712 05 35

Digital Arts & Engineering
MPEG Encoding
JPEG Encoding
CD one-offs.
Phone: (818) 791-5313
Fax: (818) 791-5510

Pacific Video Resources
MPEG1 and MPEG2 Encoding
CD-i Development
2331 Third Street
San Francisco, CA 94107
Phone: (415) 864-5679
Fax: (415) 864-2059

PLAYBACK HARDWARE FOR MPEG DIGITAL VIDEO

PC Boards for MPEG1 Playback
928 Movie with MPEG from VideoLogic
Digital Theatre from Hyundai

Matrox Marvel 2 from Matrox
Movie Master from Ace Coin
Movie Media from Micro Vitec
MPEG Master from Visionetics
ReelMagic from Sigma Designs
VideoImpact from RasterOps/Truevision

Macintosh Boards for MPEG1 Playback
Auralia board from I2M

MPEG-Compatible Game Machines
3D0 R.E.A.L Multiplayer from Panasonic
3D0 Multiplayer from Goldstar
3D0 Multiplayer from Sanyo
CD32 from Commodore
Jaguar from Atari

CD-i Players (CD-i and Video CD)
CDI450 from Magnavox
CDI550 from Magnavox
CDI220 from Philips
CDI310 Portable from Philips
CDI350 Portable from Philips
CDI605 Authoring and Reference Player from Philips
GDI-11 from Goldstar
Pro 1000 from Yashica/Kyocera

Dedicated Video CD Players
Digital Vision from JVC
CDK320 from Digital Video Systems
CDK340 from Digital Video Systems
DVC 500 RK (5 disc carousel) from Samsung
DV 530 KV Laserdisc Plus from Samsung
(Laserdisc, Karaoke and Video CD)

DIGITAL VIDEO

TITLE

DEVELOPMENT

CASE STUDY

DIGITAL VIDEO TITLE DEVELOPMENT CASE STUDY

Philips Interactive Media of America (PIMA) in Los Angeles, CA is a division of Philips NV, the consumer electronics giant of the Netherlands. PIMA has been in the business of interactive title development for CD-i for many years and was one of the very first organizations in the world to develop titles using MPEG digital video. PIMA, in cooperation with Paramount Studios produced the first digital video movies on CD-i in early 1994 in anticipation of the general release of MPEG capability in CD-i players. In late 1994, PIMA began releasing feature movies in the Video CD format for play on CD-i and Video CD players.

In this interview, we talk with Andy Davidson, Director of Engineering with the Engineering Advanced Development group at PIMA about the making of a digital video movie for Video CD. PIMA produced the Video CD version of many major motion pictures for Paramount Studios. Andy talks about each phase of the project of creating a Video CD from an existing motion picture, from analysis through final development.

Analyze

Q: Where did the idea for this project originate?

A: The idea for this project originated in-house at Philips Interactive Media of America. It was a joint effort between our Sidewalk Studio production and Engineering Advanced Development groups.

Q: What analysis was done to determine if the project was feasible?

A: As we were trying to jump-start a brand new platform and industry as a result of this project, we did as much analysis of the market as we could. However, much of it was, of necessity, speculative and based on our collective intuition and knowledge of the home video and multimedia business. On the technical side, we had much less uncertainty since we were developing a CD-i application and already had sufficient expertise in that area. [*The Video CD specification requires that each Video CD contain a CD-i application for cross-platform compatibility*]

The new technical challenge in this project was to incorporate MPEG playback into our CD-i knowledge base and to develop production expertise in preparing MPEG bitstreams from feature films.

The market analysis was spearheaded by the Sidewalk group, while Engineering provided the technical expertise.

Design

Q: How was the overall design of the project was determined and who was involved in the creative desion making?

A: As we were attempting to set a standard for a consumer user interface for digital video movies, we did very thorough and extensive design work on this project.

The first step was a storyboard effort on paper, to describe all of the various scenarios and features that should be available to the user. Following that, we did an interactive prototype using Macromedia Director, which allowed us to feel some actual interactive behavior, albeit not on the target platform. Next, we used Media Mogul to prototype the application [for CD-i]. This gave us an actual CD-i implementation fairly quickly, although not in the final style and performance. The final implementation was a custom C application.

The design team was composed of a producer, creative director, interactive design specialist, engineering manager, and graphic designer.

Produce

Q: When was the project team assembled and what disciplines were represented on the project team?

A: Following the design phase, we assembled the development team. This consisted of project manager, software engineers, graphic designers, technical writer, and production coordinator.

Q: Please describe the audio and video elements that are part of this project. What software and hardware were used to create the A/V element?

A: The titles created with this system were feature films from a major motion picture studio. In addition to the compressed digital video versions of these movies, the playback employed on-screen menus [*that function much like a book's table of contents*] to browse through the various scenes in the movies interactively. These still graphics were created individually for each title. A standard VCR-style control bar was developed to provide navigation functions and was common to all titles.

We used a service bureau to do all of the MPEG compression work. All of the graphics were created on the Mac using PhotoShop, Illustrator, and other standard desktop publishing tools and then converted to CD-i formats using OptImage plugins.

Create

Q: Did you use authoring software to develop the program logic? If not, what programming language did you use?

A: The application was developed in C and not using an authoring tool. We required the flexibility and performance afforded by custom coding. We used Philips Interactive Media internal, proprietary software that was developed in order to provide a convenient system for creating a large volume of Video CD software titles. This sofware provides a template and authoringsystem for converting feature film and music video titles to Video CD.

Validate

Q: When the title was complete, what testing methodologies did you use to validate the title? Do you employ a testing team that specializes in title testing and verification?

A: We had our internal Product Test department do a thorough validation of the template we were developing. This amounted to initially approximately 30 person-weeks of effort, followed by a few more rounds of 10 person-weeks as subsequent versions were completed. Since this was not just a single title being developed, but a template for potentially hundreds of titles, we could justify that level of effort.

The testing team has a moderately formal mechanism in place for testing interactive multimedia software. They document the title functionality, prepare a testing procedural guide, and do analysis and collating of results.

Wrap-up

Q: From analysis through initial distribution, how long did title development take:

A: A rough approximation of the development process is:

Analysis:	20%
Design:	20%
A/V production:	30%
Program.:	40%
Testing:	25%

The total is over 100% since many of these tasks overlapped in time.

Q: In general terms, how was the project budgeted?

A: Budgeting was accomplished by estimating the amount of time required for each task and phase, deciding on the team members necessary to accomplish these tasks, and coming up with the total cost of hiring these people.

Budgeting Information

When making the decision to produce digital video titles you'll be considering many options in terms of platform, equipment, and personnel. The resource guide in this book can give you a starting point for finding software, hardware, and outsource talent , but before you make the first call, you need to develop a general budget.

This chapter discusses budgeting in general terms. What isn't covered here is licensing fees. Certain authoring systems require that you own a license to produce titles. These fees can range from a one-time, unlimited license, to a per-manufactured-disc fee; some authoring systems require no liscense at all. Obviously, this issue can play a major role in the cost of development and distribution of a finished title. One of the first question you need to ask when shopping for an authoring system is "What is the liscensing agreement and how much will it cost me over time".

The costs described here are ball-park figures only. Actual costs will vary widely depending on where you buy, if you buy new or pre-owned, sales and promotions, whether you can buy systems piece by piece or a turnkey solution, and, foremost, what quality you expect to produce. Prices for computer hardware and software also tend to be very volatile. A software package priced at $3000 one day may drop to $500 the next.

Another reason for the wide variation in prices, especially with encoding systems is the variance in what a system comprises. Some encoder systems are complete turn-key encoding systems that support a wide variety of disc formats. Others may require you to make other purchases such as sound cards to complete your system, or may not encode in real time. The same is true of encoding service bureaus. The quoted price may reflect a broader service from some companies. It's important to ask lots of questions and learn as much about available products and services as possible.

Development Platform (Hardware only)

Platform	Cost
CD-ROM (PC)	$4,000-$8,000
CD-ROM (Mac)	$5,000-$10,000
CD-i	
$8,000-$18,000	
Video CD	

Authoring System (Software Only)

Platform	Cost
CD-ROM (PC)	$700-$1,500
CD-ROM (Mac)	$700-$1,500
CD-i	$7,500
Video CD	$2,000-$6,000

Encoding System

Desktop Component	$4,700-$29,995
Desktop Composite	$29,995-$75,000

Still Graphics Software

Still Image Production	$150-$600
Animation Rendering/3D Rendering	$250-$500
Image Conversion	$500-$2,500* *

Audio

Audio Capture and Digitizing	$200-$600
Audio Conversion (Compression)	$300-$3,500

Service Bureau

Encoding	$75-$300/minute

Disc Replication

Disc Replication(depends on quantity)	$1-$3/ disc

---

* Higher priced packages may offer both audio and image conversion and database.

DIGITAL VIDEO TITLES

DIGITAL VIDEO TITLES

GENERAL RELEASE ONLY

* Video CD titles (also play on CD-i)
All other titles are CD-i.

MOVIES
Patriot Games
The Hunt for Red October
Fatal Attraction
The Secret of Nimh
Wayne's World 2
Moonstruck
Robocop
Rainman
Star Trek VI: The Undiscovered Country
Apocalypse Now
Naked Gun 2 1/2
Black Rain
Top Gun
White Christmas
Indecent Proposal
Sliver
Posse

The Firm
Dr. No
From Russia with Love
Goldfinger
Dances with Wolves
The Coneheads
X-Men: Night of the Sentinels
Addams Family
Addams Family Values
Waync's World

MUSIC VIDEOS
Keep the Faith : An Evening with Bon Jovi
The Cream of Eric Clapton
Bryan Adams: Waking Up the Neighbors
Andrew Lloyd Webber: The Premier Collection
Sting: Ten Summoner's Tales
Billy Ray Cyrus: Live
*Pete Townsend Live
*Peter Gabriel: All about US
*Carreras Domingo Pavarotti:
   The Three Tenors in Concert

GAMES
Caesar's World of Boxing
Shari Lewis: Lamb Chop's Play-Along Action Songs
The Best of Baby Songs
Hanna-Barbera's Cartoon Carnival
The Seventh Guest
Mutant Rampage Bodyslam
Rebel Assault

Mad Dog McCree
Space Ace

Special Interest
Golf My Way
Tennis Our Way
Playboy: Complete Massage
Microcosm
Joy of Sex
NFL's 100 Greatest Touchdowns

Education and Training
All Time Favorite Dances ... The Best Dance Around
The Backcare Program
Carpal Tunnel Syndrome
Great American Golf 2
Interactive Math: Applied Algebra Program
Interactive Math: Basic Math Program
Interactive Science Series
Self-Breast Examination
Think and Grow Rich
Totem Poles of the West Coast
Advancing Team Performance
Confined Spaces: Training the Team
Gender in the Workplace
The Intercultural Workteam
Pass ACLS Mosby Year Book
Spine Sense
Supervisors Development Program
The Suturing Course

CD-ROM

DEVELOPERS

CD-ROM DEVELOPERS

A.D.A.M. Software, Inc.
1600 Riveredge Parkway, Suite 800
Atlanta, GA 30328
404-980-0888
404-955-3088
Developer/Publisher

ad•hoc TECHNOLOGIES, Inc.
110 Caledonia Street, Suite 2
Sausalito, CA 94965-1559
415-332-0180
415-332-0182
Developer/Publisher

Broderbund Software, Inc.
500 Redwood Boulevard
Novato, CA 94948-6121
415-382-4400
415-382-4582
Developer/Publisher

Bureau of Electronic Publishing
141 New Road
Parsippany, NJ 07054
201-808-2700
201-808-2676
Developer/Publisher

Computer Curriculum Corporation
1287 Lawrence Station Road
Sunnyvale, CA 94089
800-227-8324
408-745-6048
Developer/Publisher

Computer Directions
2712 West Shaw, Suite 234
Fresno, CA 93704
209-435-7775
209-435-3131
Developer/Publisher

CompuWorld
51, rue des Vieilles Tuileries
Gambais 78950
FRANCE
33-1-34-87-77-63
33-1-34-87-74-92
Developer/Publisher

Decision Development Corporation
2680 Bishop Drive, Suite 122
San Ramon, CA 94583
800-835-4332
510-830-0830
Developer/Publisher

DeLorme Mapping
PO Box 298, Lower Main Street
Freeport, ME 04032
207-865-1234
207-865-9291
Developer/Publisher

Dr. T's Music Software, Inc.
124 Crescent Road
Needham, MA 02194
617-455-1454
617-455-1460
Developer/Publisher

Easy Computing
Chaussée d'Alsemberg 610
Brussels 1180
BELGIUM
32-2-346-5252
32-2-346-0120
Developer/Publisher

Edmark Corp.
6727 185th Avenue, N.E.
Redmond, WA 98052
206-556-8400
206-556-8998
Developer/Publisher

EDUSOFT
132, boulevard Camélinat
Malakoff Cedex 92247
FRANCE
33-1-46-73-05-55
33-1-46-73-05-65
Developer/Publisher

ESCAPE Soft
100 East Walton, 36D
Chicago, IL 60611
312-943-6764
312-943-6765
Developer/Publisher

Falcon Software, Inc
One Hollis Street
Wellesley, MA 02181
617-235-1767
617-235-7026
Developer/Publisher

Frame Informatique SA
32 Avenue de l'Europe
Velizy 78140
FRANCE
33-1-34-88-99-99
33-1-34-88-99-34
Developer/Publisher

Future Vision Multimedia
300 Airport Executive Park
Spring Valley, NY 10977
914-426-0400
914-426-2606
Developer/Publisher

GameTek, Inc.
2999 Northeast 191st Street, 5th Floor
Aventura, FL 33180
305-935-3995
305-932-8651
Developer/Publisher

Gold Disk, Inc.
3350 Scott Boulevard, Building 14
Santa Clara, CA 95054
408-982-0200
408-982-0298
Developer/Publisher

Graphix Zone, Inc.
38 Corporate Park, Suite 100
Irvine, CA 92714
714-833-3838
714-833-3990
Developer/Publisher

HyperGlot Software Company, Inc
PO Box 10746
Knoxville, TN 37939-0746
615-558-8270
615-588-6569
Developer/Programmer

ICS Learning Systems
925 Oak Street
Scranton, PA 18515
717-342-7701
717-343-0560
Developer/Programmer

Instant Access International, Ltd.
The Technology Park, Colindeep Lane
London NW9 6DU
UK
44-81-205-2596
44-81-200-9882
Developer/Programmer
Distributor

Intellimedia Sports, Inc.
Two Piedmont Center, Suite 300
Atlanta, GA 30305-1502
404-262-0000
404-261-2282
Developer/Publisher

Interplay Productions
17922 Fitch Avenue
Irvine, CA 92714
714-553-6655
714-252-2820
Developer/Publisher

Jones Interactive, Inc.
9697 East Mineral Avenue
Englewood, CO 80155-3309
303-792-3111
303-784-8597
Developer/Publisher

JOT Publishing, Inc.
60 Bishop Drive, Suite 100
Fredericton, NB E3C 1B2
CANADA
506-459-2656
506-458-8057
Developer/Programmer

JourneyWare Media, Inc
550 Center Street, Suite 123
Moraga, CA 94556
510-254-4520
510-284-2619
Developer/Publisher

Knowledge Adventure, Inc.
4502 Dyer Street
La Crescenta, CA 91214
818-542-4200
818-542-4475
Developer/Publisher

LearningWays
161 First Street
Cambridge, MA 02142
617-576-3007
617-576-4626
Developer/Programmer

Living Books
500 Redwood Boulevard
Novato, CA 94948
415-382-4400
415-382-3030
Developer/Publisher

McGraw-Hill Professional Publishing
11 West 19th Street, 3rd Floor
New York, NY 10011
212-337-5038
212-337-5999
Developer/Publisher

Medio Multimedia, Inc.
2643-151st Place Northeast
Redmond, WA 98052-5562
206-867-5500
206-855-4142
Developer/Publisher

MicroBusiness Italiana Srl
Via G. Carducci, 125, Sesto San Giovanni
Milano 20099
ITALY
39-2-224-78033
39-2-224-78070
Developer/Publisher

Millennium Media Group, Inc.
234 North Columbus Boulevard, Third Floor
Philadelphia, PA 19106
215-625-8888
215-625-2567
Developer/Publisher

Mindscape
60 Leveroni Court
Novato, CA 94949
415-883-3000
415-883-0293
Developer/Publisher

Morris Multimedia
2707 Plaza Del Amo, Suite 601
Torrance, CA 90503
310-533-4800
310-533-1993
Developer/Publisher

MPI Multimedia
16101 South 108th Avenue
Orland Park, IL   60462
708-460-0555
708-873-3177
Developer/Programmer

Multicom Publishing, Inc.
1100 Olive Way, Suite 1250
Seattle, WA   98101
206-622-5530
206-622-4380
Developer/Publisher

Next Base Ltd.
Headline House, Chaucer Road
Ashford, Middlesex   TW15 2QT
UK
44-784-421-422
44-784-420-072
Developer/Publisher

Optical Data Corporation
30 Technology Drive
Warren, NJ   07059
908-668-0022
908-668-4929
Developer/Publisher

Overdrive Systems, Inc.
23980 Chagrin Boulevard, Suite 200
Beachwood, OH 44122-5542
216-292-3425
216-292-4888
Developer/Publisher

Pro CD, Inc.
222 Rosewood Drive
Danvers, MA 01923
508-750-0000
508-750-0020
Developer/Publisher

Putnam New Media
11490 Commerce Park Drive, Suite 130
Reston, VA 22091
703-860-3375
703-860-3620
Developer/Publisher

Q/Media Software Corporation
312 East 5th Avenue
Vancouver, BC V5T 1H4
CANADA
604-879-1190
604-879-0214
Developer/Publisher

Rainbow Technologies
122, Avenue Charles de Gaulle
Neuilly Sur Seine 95222
FRANCE
33-1-47-38-21-21
33-1-46-24-76-91
Developer/Publisher

ResourceWare Int.
Sagitalaan 7
Eindhoven 5632 AK
THE NETHERLANDS
31-40-427008/413252
31-40-427008/413252
Distributor

Scholastic Software
555 Broadway
New York, NY 10012
212-505-6006
212-353-8219
Developer/Publisher

Seminar Software, Inc
PO Box 12769
Dallas, TX 75225
214-361-4227
214-361-4227 x3*
Developer/Publisher

Sir-Tech Software, Inc.
PO Box 245
Ogdensburg, NY 13669-0245
315-393-6451
315-393-1525
Developer/Publisher

Sirius Publishing, Inc.
7320 East Butherus Drive, Suite 100
Scottsdale, AZ 85260-2438
602-951-3288
602-951-3884
Developer/Publisher

Software Sorcery
5405 Morehouse Drive, Suite 200
San Diego, CA 92121-4724
619-452-9901
619-452-5079
Developer/Publisher

Software Support, Inc.
300 International Parkway, Suite 320
Heathrow, FL 32746
407-333-4433
407-333-9080
Developer/Publisher

StarPress Multimedia, Inc.
303 Sacramento Street, Second Floor
San Francisco, CA 94111
415-274-8383
415-291-0225
Developer/Publisher

T/Maker Company
1390 Villa Street
Mountain View, CA 94041
415-962-0195
415-962-0201
Developer/Publisher

Time Warner Electronic Publishing
1271 Avenue of the Americas
New York, NY 10020
212-522-1212
212-522-7996
Developer/Publisher

Transparent Language, Inc.
22 Proctor Hill Road, PO Box 575
Hollis, NH 03049-0575
603-465-2230
603-465-2779
Developer/Publisher

Turbo Music Corporation
130 East Sixth Street
Cincinnati, OH 45202
513-381-0506
513-381-0909
Developer/Publisher

Virtual Vegas Inc.
1517 20th Street
Santa Monica, CA 90404
310-315-3606
310-453-4190
Developer/Publisher

Xaos Tools, Inc
600 Townsend, Suite 270E
San Francisco, CA 94103
415-487-7000
415-558-9886
Developer/Publisher

American Laser Games, Inc.
4801 Lincoln Road, Northeast
Albuquerque, NM 87109
505-880-1718
505-880-1557
Video Game Publisher

Children's Television Workshop
One Lincoln Plaza
New York, NY 10023
212-875-6644
212-875-6115
Developer/Publisher

Crystal Dynamics, Inc.
87 Encina Avenue
Palo Alto, CA 94301
415-473-3400
415-473-3420
Developer/Publisher

LucasArts Entertainment Company
PO Box 10307
San Rafael, CA 94912
415-721-3300
415-721-3344
Developer/Publisher

ReadySoft Inc.
3375 14th Avenue, Units 7 & 8
Markham, ON L3R OH2
CANADA
905-475-4801
905-475-4802
Developer/Publisher

T & E Soft
One Camino Sobrante, Suite 14
Orinda, CA 94563
510-253-1750
510-253-1788
Developer/Publisher

Educational Insights, Inc
19560 South Rancho Way
Dominguez Hills, CA 90220
310-637-2131
310-605-5048
Developer/Publisher

GTE Interactive Media
2385 Camino Vida Roble, Suite 200A
Carlsbad, CA 92009
619-431-8801
619-431-8755
Developer/Publisher

Philips Interactive Media
11111 Santa Monica Boulevard, Suite 400
Los Angeles, CA 90025
310-444-6600
310-478-4810
Developer/Publisher

Alliance Interactive Software
1859 North Pine Island Road, Suite 103
Plantation, FL 33322
305-423-4289
305-424-9054
Developer/Publisher

American Education Publishing
150 East Wilson Bridge Road, Suite 145
Columbus, OH 43085-2328
614-848-8866
614-848-8868
Developer/Publisher

Amtex Software Corporation
RR 2, Highway 2 West
Belleville, ON K8N 5J3
CANADA
613-967-7900
613-967-7902
Developer/Publisher

Anaya Multimedia S.A.
Juan Ignacio Luca De Tena, #15
Madrid 20827
SPAIN
34-1-320-0119
34-1-742-6631
Developer/Publisher

AT&T Multimedia Software Solutions
2701 Maidlan Center Parkway
Maidlan, FL 32751
407-662-7235
407-662-7117
Developer/Publisher

Automap, Inc.
1309 114th Avenue Southeast, Suite 110
Bellevue, WA 98004-6999
206-455-3552
206-455-3667
Developer/Publisher

Banner Blue Software
39500 Stevenson Place, Suite 204
Fremont, CA 94539
510-794-6850
510-794-9152
Developer/Publisher

Bantam Doubleday Dell Publishing Group
1540 Broadway, 15th Floor
New York, NY 10036
212-782-8768
212-782-8338
Developer/Publisher

BayWare, Inc.
1660 South Amphlett Boulevard, Suite 128
San Mateo, CA 94402
415-286-4480
415-578-1884
Developer/Publisher

BBN Systems & Technologies
150 Cambridge Park Drive
Cambridge, MA 02140
617-873-3081
617-873-2455
Developer/Publisher

Bethesda Softworks
1370 Piccard Drive, Suite 120
Rockville, MD 20850-4304
301-926-8300
301-926-8010
Developer/Publisher

Byron Preiss Multimedia Co.
24 West 25th Street, 11th Floor
New York, NY 10010
212-989-6252
212-989-6550
Developer/Publisher

Cambium Development, Inc.
Post Office Box 296-H
Scarsdale, NY 10583-8796
914-472-6246
914-472-6729
Developer/Publisher

The Cute Company
P.O. Box 529
Canton, CT 06019
203-693-2399
203-693-4173
Developer/Publisher

Davidson & Associates
19840 Pioneer Avenue
Torrance, CA 90503
310-793-0600
310-793-0601
Developer/Publisher

DINE Systems, Inc.
586 North French Road, Suite 2
Amherst, NY 14228-9965
716-688-2400
716-688-2505
Developer/Publisher

Discovery Communications, Inc
7700 Wisconsin Avenue
Bethesda, MD 20814-3522
301-986-1999
301-986-4827
Developer/Publisher

Don Johnston, Inc.
1000 North Rand Road, Building 115, PO Box 639
Wauconda, IL 60084
708-526-2682
708-526-4177
Developer/Publisher

Dorling Kindersley Publishing, Inc.
95 Madison Avenue, Tenth Floor
New York, NY 10017
212-213-4800
212-213-5202
Developer/Publisher

Educational Resources
1550 Executive Drive
Elgin, IL 60123
708-888-8300
708-888-8689
Developer/Publisher

Epic MegaGames
3204 Tower Oaks Boulevard, Suite 410
Rockville, MD 20852
301-468-6012
301-299-3841
Developer/Publisher

Expert Software, Inc.
800 Douglas Road, Executive Tower, Suite 750
Coral Gables, FL 33134-3128
305-567-9990
305-443-0786
Developer/Publisher

Expert's Choice Software
4612 Trail West
Austin, TX 78735
512-422-1622
512-892-5453
Developer/Publisher

Frame Technology
The Arena Forum, Stockley Park Business Centre
Uxbridge, Middlesex UB11 1AA
UK
44-81-899-1721
44-81-899-1732
Developer/Publisher

General Media International/Omni Publications
1965 Broadway
New York, NY 10023
212-496-6100
212-580-3693
Developer/Publisher

Global Interactive Corporation
12121 Wilshire Boulevard, Suite 1020
Los Angeles, CA 90025
310-820-4200
310-826-6243
Developer/Publisher

Great Bear Technology Incorporated
1100 Moraga Way, Suite 101
Moraga, CA 94556
510-631-1600
510-631-6735
Developer/Publisher

Grolier Educational Corporation
Sherman Turnpike
Danbury, CT 06816
203-797-3500
203-797-3285
Developer/Publisher

Grolier Electronic Publishing, Inc.
Sherman Turnpike
Danbury, CT 06816
203-797-3530
203-797-3835
Developer/Publisher

Harper Collins Publishers
10 East 53rd Street, 21st Floor
New York, NY 10022
212-207-7000
212-207-7433
Developer/Publisher

Headbone Interactive
1520 Bellevue Avenue
Seattle, WA 98122-9952
206-323-0073
206-323-0188
Developer/Publisher

Husdawg Enterprises, Inc.
336 Sixth Street
San Francisco, CA 94103
415-241-9214
415-252-5570
Developer/Publisher

In4mation Software
208 West Paseo De Cristobal
San Clemente, CA 92672-5433
714-366-1115
714-366-1405
Developer/Publisher

Index Stock Photography, Inc.
126 Fifth Avenue, 7th Floor
New York, NY 10011
212-929-4644
212-633-1914
Developer/Publisher

Individual Software Inc.
5870 Stoneridge Drive, Suite 1
Pleasanton, CA 94588
510-734-6767
510-734-8337
Developer/Publisher

Intersound Inc.
PO Box 1724
Roswell, GA 30077
404-664-9262
404-664-7316
Developer/Publisher

IntraCorp Inc.
7200 Northwest 19th Street, Suite 500
Miami, FL 33126
305-591-5900
305-591-1561
Developer/Publisher

Intuit
PO Box 3014
Menlo Park, CA 94026-3014
415-322-0573
415-329-3655
Developer/Publisher

I•Motion, Inc
1333 Ocean Avenue, Suite J
Santa Monica, CA 90401
310-576-1888
310-576-1889
Developer/Publisher

Jostens Learning Corporation
9920 Pacific Heights Boulevard, Suite 100
San Diego, CA 92121
619-587-0087
619-587-1629
Developer/Publisher

KidSoft, Inc
718 University Avenue, Suite 112
Los Gatos, CA 95030-3313
408-354-6100
408-354-1033
Developer/Publisher

Larousse Multimedia
5, Square Max Hymans
Paris 75015
FRANCE
33-1-44-39-42-39
33-1-44-39-43-95
Developer/Publisher

Legacy Software
8521 Reseda Boulevard
Northridge, CA 91324
818-885-5773
818-885-5779
Developer/Publisher

Legend Entertainment Company
14200 Park Meadow Drive
Chantilly, VA 22021
703-222-8500
703-968-5151

Developer/Publisher

LIST Services, Inc.
15012 Wycliffe Drive, Suite 23
Omaha, NE 68022
402-334-4991
402-691-8670
Developer/Publisher

Lucid Corporation
101 West Renner Road, Suite 450
Richardson, TX 75082-2017
214-994-8100
214-994-8103
Developer/Publisher

Lurie, Debevetz & Associates, Inc.
4815 South Harvard, Suite 350
Tulsa, OK 74135
918-743-8881
918-745-6688
Developer/Publisher

Lyriq International Corporation
1701 Highland Avenue
Cheshire, CT 06410
203-250-2070
203-250-2072
Developer/Publisher

Macmillan/McGraw-Hill School Division
1221 Avenue of the Americas
New York, NY 10020
212-512-6619
212-512-6334
Developer/Publisher

Marketing Directions, Inc.
7805 Telegraph Road, Suite 215
Minneapolis, MN 55438
612-944-6805
612-944-1704
Developer/Publisher

MarketPlace Information Corporation
460 Totten Pond Road
Waltham, MA 02154-1906
617-672-9200
617-672-9290
Developer/Publisher

Masque Publishing
7006 South Alton Way, Building A
Englewood, CO 80112
303-290-9853
303-290-6303
Developer/Publisher

MECC
6160 Summit Drive North
Minneapolis, MN 55430-4003
612-569-1500
612-569-1551
Developer/Publisher

The MEDVEC Company
151 Kentucky Avenue, Southeast
Washington, DC 20003-1447
202-546-1220
202-547-5476
Developer/Publisher

Megatech Software
1606 Lockness Place
Torrance, CA 90501
310-539-6452
310-539-8450
Developer/Publisher

Merit Studios
13707 Gamma Road
Dallas, TX 75244-4409
214-385-2353
214-385-8205
Developer/Publisher

Merriam-Webster, Inc.
47 Federal Street, PO Box 281
Springfield, MA 01102
413-734-3134
413-731-5979
Developer/Publisher

Micrografx, Inc.
1303 East Arapaho Road
Richardson, TX 75081
214-234-1769
214-994-6475
Developer/Publisher

Mission Studios, Corp.
1644 Colonial Parkway
Inverness, IL 60067
708-991-0598
708-991-4408
Developer/Publisher

Moon Valley Software
141 Suburban Road, Suite A1
San Luis Obispo, CA 93401
805-781-3890
805-781-3898
Developer/Publisher

Morris Multimedia Interactive
2707 Plaza Del Amo, Suite 601
Torrance, CA 90503
310-533-4800
310-533-1993
Developer/Publisher

News Electronic Data, Inc.
28 Center Street
Clinton, NJ 08809
908-735-2555
908-735-8113
Developer/Publisher

Nordic Software, Inc.
6911 Van Dorn/PO Box 6007
Lincoln, NE 68506-0007
402-488-5086
402-488-2914
Developer/Publisher

NovaLogic, Inc.
26010 Mureau Road, Suite 200
Calabasas, CA 91302
818-880-1997
818-880-1998
Developer/Publisher

PWA, Inc.
60 West 85th Street, Suite B
New York, NY 10024
212-769-1209
212-787-0581
Developer/Publisher

SelectWare Technologies, Inc.
29200 Vassar Street, Suite 200
Livonia, MI 48152
810-477-7340
810-477-6488
Developer/Publisher

Softissimo
9, rue Scribe
Paris 75005
FRANCE
33-1-43-12-85-00
33-1-42-66-11-54
Developer/Publisher

Softprime, Inc.
500 Kirts Boulevard
Troy, MI 48084
810-362-4400
810-362-5166
Developer/Publisher

Software Holdings, Inc.
1750 NW 65th Avenue
Plantation, FL 33313
305-583-8897
305-583-8767
Developer/Publisher

Sony Imagesoft
2400 Broadway Avenue, Suite 550
Santa Monica, CA 90404
310-449-2999
310-449-2412
Developer/Publisher

Spectrum HoloByte, Inc.
2490 Mariner Square Loop
Alameda, CA 94501
510-522-3584
510-522-2138
Developer/Publisher

Steck-Vaughn Publishing Corporation
8701 North Mopac Expressway, Suite 200
Austin, TX 78759
512-343-8227
512-795-3676
Developer/Publisher

Tadpole Productions
13100 Worldgate Drive, Suite 250
Herndon, VA 22070-4382
703-471-7453
703-471-1126
Developer/Publisher

United American Video Corporation
2100 Carolina Place
Fort Mill, SC 29715
803-548-7300
803-548-3335
Developer/Publisher

Velocity, Inc.
Four Embarcadero Center, Suite 3100
San Francisco, CA 94111-4106
415-776-8000
415-776-8099
Developer/Publisher

Vertigo Development Group
58 Charles Street
Cambridge, MA 02141
617-225-2065
617-225-0637
Developer/Publisher

Viacom New Media
1515 Broadway
New York, NY 10036
212-258-6000
212-258-6497
Developer/Publisher

Videodiscovery, Inc.
1700 Westlake Avenue North, Suite 600
Seattle, WA 98109-3012
206-285-5400
206-285-9245
Developer/Publisher

Virtual Entertainment, Inc.
200 Highland Avenue
Needham, MA 02194
617-449-7567
617-449-4887
Developer/Publisher

Western Publishing Company, Inc.
1220 Mound Avenue
Racine, WI 53404
414-633-2431
414-631-5173
Developer/Publisher

Westwood Studios
5333 South Arville, Suite #104
Las Vegas, NV 89118-2226
702-368-4850
702-368-0677
Developer/Publisher

William K. Bradford Publishing Company
16 Craig Road
Acton, MA 01720
508-263-6996
508-263-9375
Developer/Publisher

World Book Publishing
525 West Monroe Street, 20th Floor
Chicago, IL 60661
312-258-3700
312-258-3950
Developer/Publisher

Zelos
535 Pacific Avenue
San Francisco, CA 94133
415-788-0566
415-788-0562
DEVELOPER/PUBLISHER
Developer/Publisher

RECOMMENDED
READING

RECOMMENDED READING

SPECIFICATIONS
MPEG System Specification (ISO 11172-1)
MPEG Video Specification (ISO 11172-2)
MPEG Audio Specification (ISO 11172-3)
ISO specifications can be ordered from your national standards issuersuch as the American National Standards Institute (ANSI) in the U.S.

American National Standards Institute
1430 Broadway
New York, NY 10018
Phone: (212) 642-4900

MAGAZINE ARTICLES
"Walking the Labyrinth of Multimedia Law," Pamela S. Helyar and Gregory M. Doudnikoff, STC Technical Communication, *Journal of the Society for Technical Communication*, Volume 41, Number 4, November 1994, ISSN 0049-3155

"Video CD, The Technology, and The Market: Dreaming of a White Book Christmas," Mark Fritz, *CD-ROM Professional*, Volume 7 - Number 4, July-August 1994, ISSN 1049-0833

"MPEG Q&A," Matthew R. Leek, *CD-ROM Professional*, Volume 7 - Number 4, July-August 1994, ISSN 1049-0833

"Video CD, The Next Digital Format Revolution?" Daniel Greenberg, *Digital Video Magazine*, January 1995, ISSN 1075-251X

OTHER WORKS
"Interactive Optical Technologies in Education and Training," a paper written by Ben Roach, Ph.D., Association for Managerial, Professional, and Executive Development, Ltd., 5696 Peachtree Parkway, Atlanta, Georgia 30092, (404) 242-2626

"Compact Disc Technology," a technical manual on disc layouts and architecture, Disc Manufacturing, Inc., (800) 433-DISC or fax (302) 479-2527

"MPEG Frequently Asked Questions (FAQ)," electronic document and part of a FAQ on digital compression, written by Mark Adler. Available on the Internet via anonymous ftp at: ftp.uu.net in usenet/new.answers/compression-faq or World Wide Web at: ftp://ftp.uu.net/usenet/new.answers/compression-faq

GLOSSARY

GLOSSARY

Anti-Aliasing
A process that involves smoothing the jagged edges that plague digital artwork, especially text. This process is an option available in many computer paint software packages.

Aspect Ratio
The ratio of the height of a pixel to its width. Different video formats have different aspect ratios.

Authoring
A process of combining all of the screen images, digital video, and audio with programing instructions into a working title. Authoring software enables you to structure the title without using complex programming languages.

Bandwidth
The allowable amount of data that can be transferred in a given time. Typically expressed in bits per second. Bandwidth is usually a characteristic of hardware.

Bit Rate
The expected or required speed at which data is transferred. Typically expressed in bits per second. Bit rate is a characteristic of digital data.

Branching
When a multimedia application moves from one linear sequence to another.

CD-i
Compact Disc–interactive. An interactive multimedia format developed by Philips NV and Sony.

CD-ROM
Compact Disc–Read Only Memory. A compact disc that stores computer data.

Component Video
Carries the separate red, green and blue (RGB) or separate luminence and chrominance components (YUV) of the video signal on three separate input wires. Preferred video source since the three signals contain a large amount of high-quality video information.

Composite Video
A single video signal on a single wire that is a composite of all video information. Somewhat lower quality than component video since it contains less total video information, but still quite acceptable for many uses.

Compression
Digital coding method that reduces the amount of data needed to store images or sound. Minimizes redundant data by recording the first block of visual data then records only the changes in the blocks to follow.

Disc Image
A computer file that is a byte by byte representation of a disc.

Emulation
A playback environment that precisely mimics the host platform. Used to test CD titles before the CD is pressed.

GOP
Group of Pictures. A defined group of I-, P-, and B-frames preceded with complete timestamp information.

Green Book
CD-i specification. The Green Book specifies disc layout, acceptable audio and video file types, players speed, and disc layout.

Interactive TV
A combination of computers and cable TV that allows TV viewers to interact in real time with the program.

Interactivity
The exchange of information between the viewer and the multimedia application. In an interactive application, the user can control such things as pace, direction, and content.

Macro block
An 8 pixel by 8 pixel block of video.

Mastering
The process of assembling all of the individual title elements into a disc image.

Menu
List of available choices or options. A menu is a still video image with the options enclosed in interactive "hotspots."

MPEG
Motion Picture Experts Group.

MPEG1
Standard developed by the Motion Picture Experts Group that describes the decompression of audio/video data for full-screen, full-motion digital video play from a single speed compact disc. Detailed in ISO 11172.

MPEG2
Standard developed by the Motion Picture Experts Group that describes the decompression of audio/video data for full-screen, full-motion digital video play from a computer server for interactive TV.

Multimedia
Presentations combining several types of media including still video, audio, text, and motion video. Interactive multimedia requires the involvement of the viewer in the presentation.

Multiplex
To combine two or more separate data streams into a single data stream. Also known as "mux."

NTSC (National Television Standards Committee)
NTSC is the color standard for broadcast TV and video pictures in North America, Japan, and their dependents. Requires a picture size of 352 X 240 pixels and a frame rate of 30 frames per second.

PAL (Phase Alternating Line)
The color standard for broadcast TV and video pictures in the United Kingdom, most of Europe, Australia, and

South America. Requires a picture size of 384 X 280 pixels and a frame rate of 25 frames per second.

Pixel
A picture element that is the smallest element of an image that can be identified or manipulated.

Real time
Refers to activity that occurs according to the clock. Real time encoding means that one hour of video will encode in one hour.

Red Book
Audio CD specification. The Red Book specifies disc layout, player speed, and all ancillary files that must be included on an audio CD.

Replication
Mass duplication.

Safe Area
The area of a television screen where visibility of text and graphics is guaranteed. The NTSC safe area is a 320 X 210 pixel area centered on the screen. The PAL safe area is a 320 X 250 pixel area centered on the screen.

Scripting
A multimedia script is a simple list of commands that mastering software uses to build a multimedia title in the final format prior to recording a disc.

Sequence Header
Generated automatically by the encoder and contains information such as the size of the video, the video format,

and delivery rate. It always precedes the first video frame and can precede each I-frame. The sequence header must precede any I-frame identified as an entry point.

Source Video
The original, edited, analog video recording from which all subsequent copies or conversions are made.

Timestamp
In a GOP, the timestamp contains absolute time information relative to the start of the MPEG stream. In an individual video frame or audio sample, the timestamp specifies the order of the frames in the group of pictures.

Validation
The process of testing the final application just prior to disc replication and distribution.

Video CD
A compact disc format for MPEG-encoded digital video. Allows for limited interactivity. Based on the Karaoke format and governed by the Video CD specification (White Book).

Video On Demand
Service of interactive TV that allows viewers to choose a movie or music video from a menu for immediate play.

White Book
Video CD specification. The White Book is fundamentally an extension of the Red Book with additions to address still and motion video file types, player speed and bandwidth, and interactivity.

WORM

Write Once–Read Many compact disc. A blank compact disc that can be used with a CD recorder. Sometimes called a check disc or write-once disc.

AVAILABLE
FROM
MICHAEL
WIESE
PRODUCTIONS

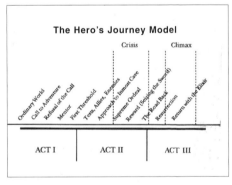

SOFTWARE

MovieMagic: Budgeting
Regular Price: ~~$595~~
MWP Price: $385

MovieMagic represents a major leap forward in budgeting software. Fast and flexible, MOVIE MAGIC: BUDGETING has become the industry standard for producers, production managers, and estimators and other film professionals. Features include: "What-if" Functions, Database of rates, Globals for speedy entry, instant recalculation, chart of accounts, etc.

Requires:
Macintosh
•MacPlus or better including Classic, Classic II, SE, SE30, II, IIILC, IIX, IICX, IISI, IIci, IIfx, Quadras, Performas, Notebooks, etc.
•Minimum 512K RAM memory, 4 Megabytes (or more) recommended for use with System 7.
•Minimum system 6.0.5 or higher. System 7-friendly.
•Two disk drives; one may be a hard disk. •Any Macintosh compatible printer & most serial printers.
IBM
•Any IBM compatible with 384K RAM memory •DOS 3.1 or higher; DOS 5.0 recommended.
•Two disk drives; one may be a hard disk.
•A printer; it can be a dot matrix, daisy-wheel or laser printer. The printer must be able to print condensed fonts (15 to 17 characters per inch) or elite fonts (12 characters per inch).

FilmProfit
MWP PRICE: $99

Created by the former CFO of Lucasfilm, FILMPROFIT is a dynamic new spreadsheet program for the MAC or PC which enables you to track cash flow through all phases of distribution and generate reports for business plans and investor presentations. Features include: Income Revenue Projections for film, TV, home video, and foreign markets, "What If" Scenarios, Calculation of Distribution Fees, Producer's Financial Reports, etc. Great for business plans and projections!

Special Bonus! Includes a <u>free</u> 100 page book titled, *The User's Guide to Film Distribution.*

Requires:
Macintosh •Hard disk • Microsoft Excel 3.0 or higher
PC •500K hard disk •DOS version 2.1 or higher

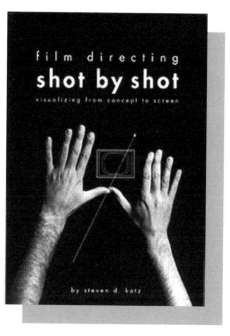

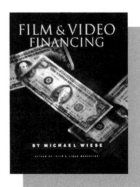

ORDER FORM

To order these products please call 1-800-379-8808 or fax (818) 986-3408 or mail this order form to:

MICHAEL WIESE PRODUCTIONS
4354 Laurel Canyon Blvd., Suite 234
Studio City, CA 91604
1-800-379-8808

BOOKS:

_____

_____

_____

_____

Subtotal $_____
Shipping $_____
8.25% Sales Tax (Ca Only) $_____

TOTAL ENCLOSED_____

Please make check or money order payable to
Michael Wiese Productions

(Check one) ____ Master Card ____Visa _____Amex

Company PO#_____

Credit Card Number_____
Expiration Date_____
Cardholder's Name_____
Cardholder's Signature_____

SHIP TO:
Name_____
Address_____
City_____State_____Zip_____
Country_____Telephone_____

Please inquire about discounts for organizations and groups. Special prices for professors and classroom adoptions.

Please allow 2-3 weeks for delivery.

CREDIT CARD ORDERS

CALL 1-800-379-8808

OR **FAX YOUR ORDER**

818 986-3408

SHIPPING

1ST CLASS MAIL
One Book - $5.00
Two Books - $7.00
For each additional book, add $1.00.

AIRBORNE EXPRESS
2nd Day Delivery
Add an additional $11.00 per order.

OVERSEAS (PREPAID)
Surface - $7.00 ea. book
Airmail - $15.00 ea. book